# Special C...

## Chocolate & clementine pudding

FAMILY FAVOURITES

Sainsbury's
live well for less

First Published 2014

Copyright © 2014 Lynette Fisher

All rights reserved. Copyright under International and Pan-American Copyright Conventions.

No part of this book may be reproduced, stored in a retrieval system or transmitted in any other form or by any other means, electronic, mechanical, photocopying, recording or otherwise without the prior permission of the publisher and copyright holder. Within the UK, exceptions are allowed in respect of any fair dealing for the purpose of research or private study, or criticism or review, as permitted under the Copyright, Designs and Patents Act, 1988.

While the publisher makes every effort possible to publish full and correct information in this book, sometimes errors of omission or substance may occur. For this the publisher is most regretful, but hereby must disclaim any liability.

ISBN 978-0-9927400-1-6

Published by Le Vieux Four Publishing, Beaminster, Dorset

Design and typesetting by Moira Read, Border Typesetting, Beaminster

Photographs and illustrations by the Author

Printed in Great Britain by iprint, Leicester

# Dedication

*For my dearest father Hervey and his caring wife (and servant) Molly. This book will always remind me of the precious time we spent together at Boturnell Farm in Cornwall, where with peace and quiet, (well apart from the cockerels, chipmunks and all the rest of the menagerie there) and many long dog walks I set out this book and typed the recipes.*

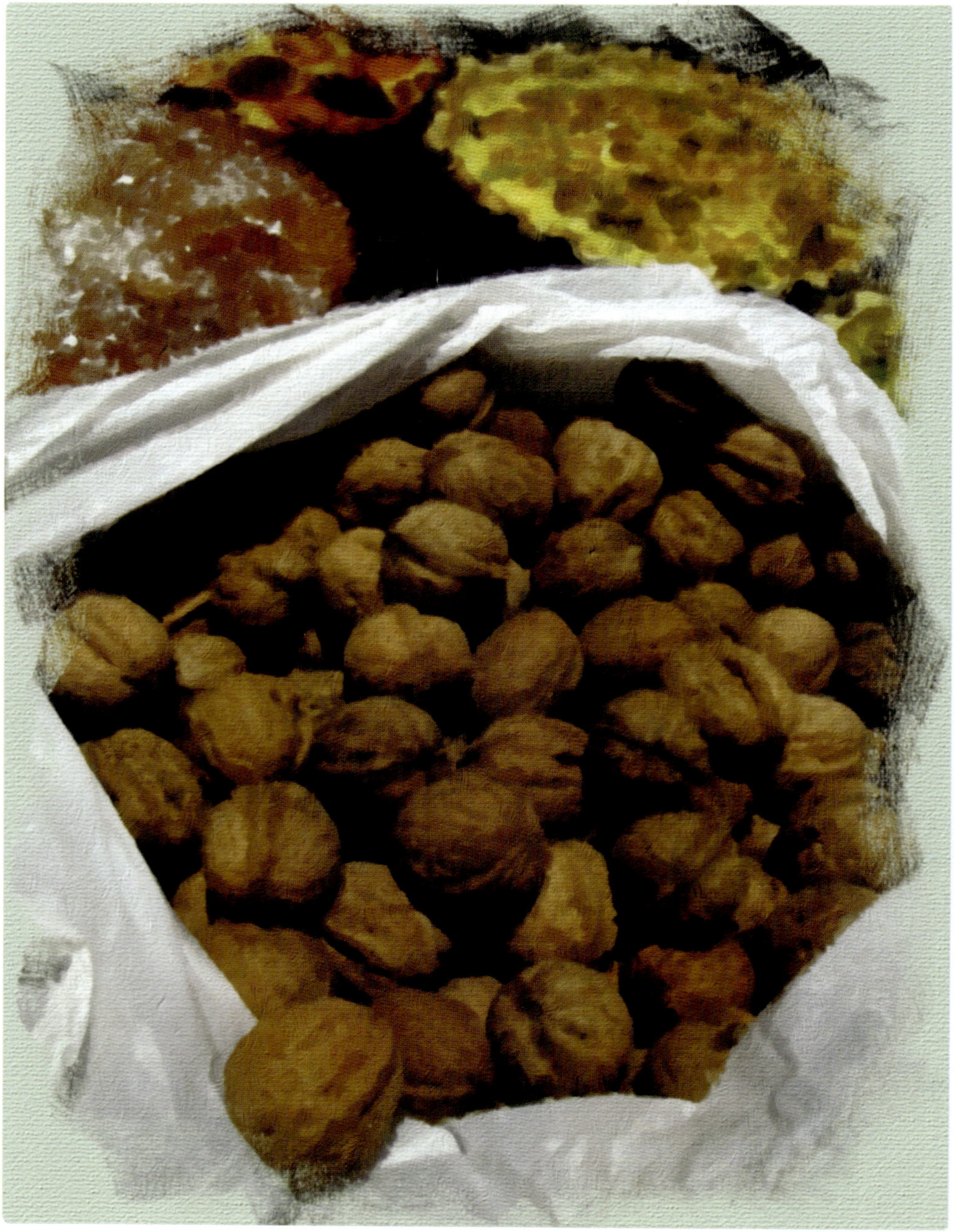

# Contents

| | |
|---|---|
| Introduction | viii |
| Acknowledgements | ix |
| Tips from my Culinary Sketch Book | x |
| Oven Temperatures | xv |

## *Le Vieux Four* SPECIALITY CAKES

| | |
|---|---|
| Black Cow Vodka Cake, with Prunes, Orange & White Chocolate | 2 |
| Winter Cake | 4 |
| Apricot Chocolate Cake, with Pistachio & Almond | 6 |
| Pear and Hazelnut Crumble Cake | 8 |
| Spice Cake with Orange Jam | 10 |
| Coffee Walnut Cake | 12 |
| Whisky-Rich Fruit Cake with Walnut Brittle | 14 |
| Lavender & Almond Lemon Drizzle | 16 |
| Caribbean Cake | 18 |

## FRESH FRUITY CAKES

| | |
|---|---|
| Fig Cake, with Honey and Orange | 22 |
| Plum Cake, with Almonds & Kirsch | 24 |
| Blood Orange & Rhubarb Loaf | 26 |
| Summer Fruit Mini Loaves | 28 |
| Black & White Pineapple Cake | 31 |
| Lemon Cake with Fresh Rhubarb Compote | 32 |

| | |
|---|---|
| Apple Strudel | 34 |
| Fresh Raspberry & Marzipan Towers | 37 |
| Roast Apricot Dacquoise with Vanilla Rice | 38 |
| Savarin with White Grapes & Kirsch | 41 |
| Soft Rum Cake with Crème Patissière & Cherry Coulis | 42 |
| Blackberry & Apple Cake with Almonds | 44 |

## VEGETABLE CAKES

| | |
|---|---|
| Pumpkin Cake | 48 |
| Beetroot Cake with Ginger, Mascarpone Icing with Fresh Raspberries | 50 |
| Sweet Potato Cake | 52 |
| Courgette, Cocoa & Hazelnut Sponge | 54 |
| Spicy Squash Mini Loaves with Sunflower Kernels & Pumpkin Seeds | 56 |
| Fennel Cake, with Crème Patissière & Fresh Apricots | 58 |

## OLD FASHIONED FRENCH RECIPES

| | |
|---|---|
| Biscuit de Savoie | 62 |
| Gateau Basque aux Cerises Noir | 64 |
| Fouace | 66 |
| Paris-Brest | 68 |
| Tropézienne | 70 |
| Pastis des Landes | 72 |
| Forêt Noire | 75 |
| Dacquoise aux Pistaches | 76 |

## CAKES WITH DRIED FRUITS, NUTS AND SEEDS

| | |
|---|---|
| *Le Vieux Four's* Lorimer Plum Cake with Guinness | 80 |
| Lemon Whiskey Cake | 82 |
| Kouglof | 84 |
| Seed cake | 86 |
| Hazelnut & Coffee Cake with Chocolate Sauce | 88 |
| Bara Brith | 90 |
| Nut Cake with Brandy | 92 |
| Earl Grey Tea Loaf | 94 |

## SIMPLE RICH CHOCOLATE CAKES FROM *Le Vieux Four*

| | |
|---|---|
| Chocolate, Cocoa & Almond Cake | 98 |
| Very Chocolatey Dark Chocolate Cake | 100 |
| Chocolate Cake with Rum | 102 |
| Chocolate Cake with Espresso & Ground Almonds | 104 |
| Chocolate Crown | 106 |
| Brownies with Pistachio & Pepper Cream Sauce | 109 |

| | |
|---|---|
| **Bibliography** | 110 |
| **Index** | 111 |

# An Adventure with Flavour and Colour

*Le Vieux Four* translates, of course, as *The Old Oven*. Many have asked if there is indeed an old oven here in my patisserie in Beaminster. The title now, on reflection, has to be awarded to the old fan assisted oven that has baked ceaselessly for me for the last twenty three years. My late stepfather went to an auction at a pub called 'The World's End' that had most unfortunately burnt to the ground, and returned with a huge stainless steel fridge and an oven, both filthy and badly damaged by the smoke.

Very little money changed hands as I remember and the appliances cleaned up beautifully and were soon restored to fine working order. The fridge passed away after a few years to be replaced with something a little more modern and economical but the oven lives on and on and very rarely has a day off. In fact it stands the pace a lot more effortlessly than the cook, who after all these years has developed a few malfunctions.

In 2008 or thereabouts I opened up the old fire place in the shop concealed for over a hundred years behind the wall. We can imagine the residents of Beaminster standing around this huge, open fire over two hundred years ago, so this feature perhaps deserves to share the title of '*The Old Oven*'.

A note from Mrs Beeton 'Cakes cost less when made at home… as much as a shilling on a large fruit cake.'

# Acknowledgements

*I should like to thank my army of cake testers who are never far away, forks poised, ready with their critique to perfect the recipes. Also those who by preordering copies before the book was hardly begun, have hastened my progress towards the finish line.*

*Special thanks to Moira Read, Sally Parker and Marion Taylor, each of whom taught me so much first time round that I actually believe I am getting better at this, but of course the proof will be in the pudding.*

*I have also to acknowledge the whippets who have followed me, drooling and mystified, as I carry my cakes around house and garden to find the right flower or perfect place for a photo.*

# Tips from my Culinary Sketch Book

*I always have a bowl of fresh, free range eggs on the side in the kitchen, as to mix and blend easily they need to be at room temperature.*

*Choose tins and moulds carefully, changing shapes to suit occasions, but watch cooking times, longer for larger, shorter for smaller.*

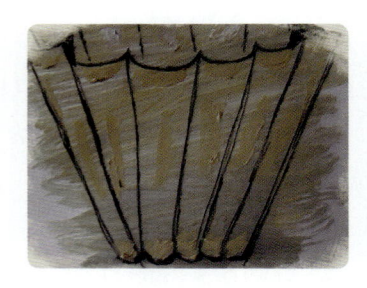

*To prevent cakes from sticking to the more ornate tins, butter them very thoroughly and then sprinkle with sieved flour tipping away the excess.*

*Increase the height of your cakes to impress with a rim of bakewell paper that rises above the edge of the tin and avoid ugly tops and wastage.*

*Always use the very best chocolate.*

*My favourite kitchen tool.*

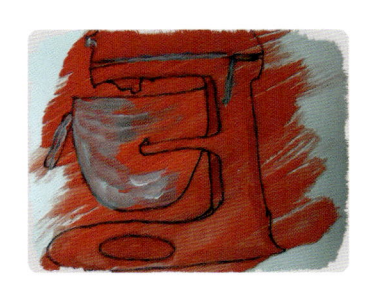

*Pick over your dried fruits carefully, I once found a small metal screw amongst dried cranberries.*

*Roast or blanche nuts to remove bitter skins.*

*Wash vegetables for the cakes and dry the grated flesh thoroughly with a paper towel.*

*Sieve your plums, cherries and damsons through a nylon sieve when making coulis.*

*Make sure your lavender is completely dry before storing in a jar.*

*Always have the right implements to hand, my pallet knife particularly, is never far away.*

*Experiment with flavours of your own.*

*Use seasonal fruits where possible for freshness and price.*

*Guinness makes a wonderful addition to dark rich fruit cakes.*

xiv   *Introduction*

# Oven Temperatures

*A word about oven temperatures.... every single oven is a different beast but hopefully in time we build a good relationship with the one we use everyday, as for successful cake baking, this is how it must be with little room for error.*

*I use gas, alongside fan-assisted electric and an Aga – and I have to say that the gas oven is the most trusted with my cakes. Always preheat the oven so that the cake goes in at the temperature that it needs. The middle shelf is always the safest place, avoiding a burnt crusty top on your creation.*

*My terms for cake temperatures translate as such, I never actually really know the temperature of the old ovens that I use!*

**Cool**                 lowest setting
**Moderate**         150°C / Gas Mark 3
**Moderately hot** 170°C–190°C / Gas Mark 4–5
**Hot**                  220°C / Gas Mark 6

LE VIEUX FOUR S

# SPECIALITY CAKES

Black Cow Vodka Cake

Winter Cake

Apricot Chocolate Cake

Pear & Hazelnut Crumble Cake

Spice Cake with Orange Jam

Coffee Walnut Cake

Whisky-Rich Fruit Cake

Lavender & Almond Lemon Drizzle

Caribbean Cake

# Black Cow Vodka Cake with Prunes, Orange & White Chocolate

*A recipe that I have devised for perhaps the most startling product to emerge from Dorset during recent years. A wonderful, smooth vodka distilled from cows' milk.*

8 dried prunes
1 large orange
150g white chocolate chips
200g caster sugar

200g butter
200g self-raising flour
4 eggs
2 tbsp of Black Cow Vodka

Grease and line a 24cm deep cake tin.

Soak the pitted prunes in the vodka for a few hours. Drain reserving the vodka for the cake and chop the prunes into small pieces.

Cream the butter and sugar until white, add the beaten eggs alternately with the flour and finally, add the chopped prunes, reserving a spoonful for the top of the cake, the chocolate chips, the vodka and the zest of the orange. Spread evenly in the tin and bake in the centre of a moderate oven.

When the cake has set, remove from the oven and sprinkle with the reserved prune and finely sliced segments of orange. Replace in the oven and continue to bake until firm to the touch and softly brown. Serve with crème fraîche.

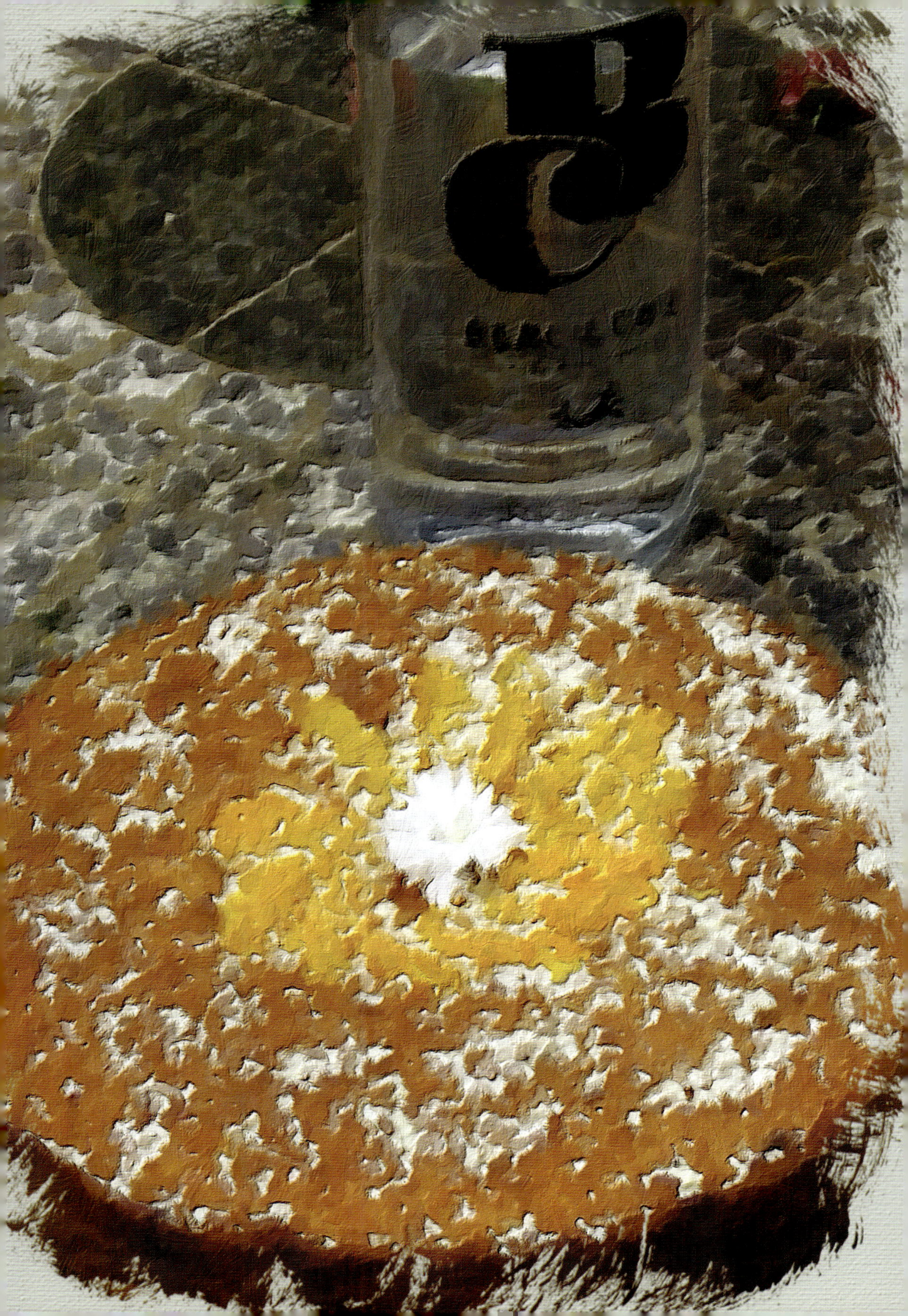

# Winter Cake

*This cake has now graduated from a 'winter cake' to an 'all the year round cake' and has in fact recently been elevated to 'Lynette's signature cake'. There are never any slices lingering for the following day.*

½ bramley apple
75g dried cranberries
75g sultanas
75g Belgian chocolate chips
2 tbsp Mount Gay rum
½ tsp grated nutmeg

200g butter
100g dark brown sugar
100g light brown sugar
4 eggs
200g self-raising flour
100g marzipan

Grease and line a 24cm deep cake tin.

Peel and chop the apple in small pieces, place in a bowl with the cranberries, sultanas, chocolate chips and rum and put on one side to marinate while the rest of the cake is prepared.

Cream the sugars with the butter until well blended and add the eggs alternately with the flour. Add the fruit mixture with the rum and the grated nutmeg. Spread half in the tin and then rolling the marzipan out to a thin round, place on top followed by the rest of the cake mixture. Bake in the centre of a moderate oven until risen, brown and firm to the touch.

Allow to cool and decorate with drizzled, melted chocolate and thin, crystallised slices of apple and chopped cranberry, placing these on before the chocolate cools and hardens.

# Chocolate Cake with Pistachio, Apricot & Almond

*A rich, moist, delicious chocolate cake, refined for cake experts who enjoy something a little unexpected!*

**260g soft butter**
**400g icing sugar**
**2 egg yolks plus 4 eggs**
**100ml milk**
**300g self-raising flour**
**80g cocoa powder**
**250g sliced tinned apricots**
**150g chopped pistachios (unsalted)**
**150g chopped whole almonds**
**150g raisins**

Line a 25cm tin with butter and baking parchment.

Mix the butter with the sugar until creamy and white.

Add the egg yolks and then the whole eggs and the milk, mixing in some of the flour if the mixture tends to curdle, followed by all of the flour and the cocoa powder. Mix in the fruits and nuts reserving a few to decorate the top. Spread the mixture evenly in the prepared tin and bake in the centre of a moderate oven. When the cake is risen and set but not fully baked scatter on the reserved nuts and slices of apricot, and replace in the oven until the cake is firm to the to the touch.

A sprinkle of home made golden praline is perfection.

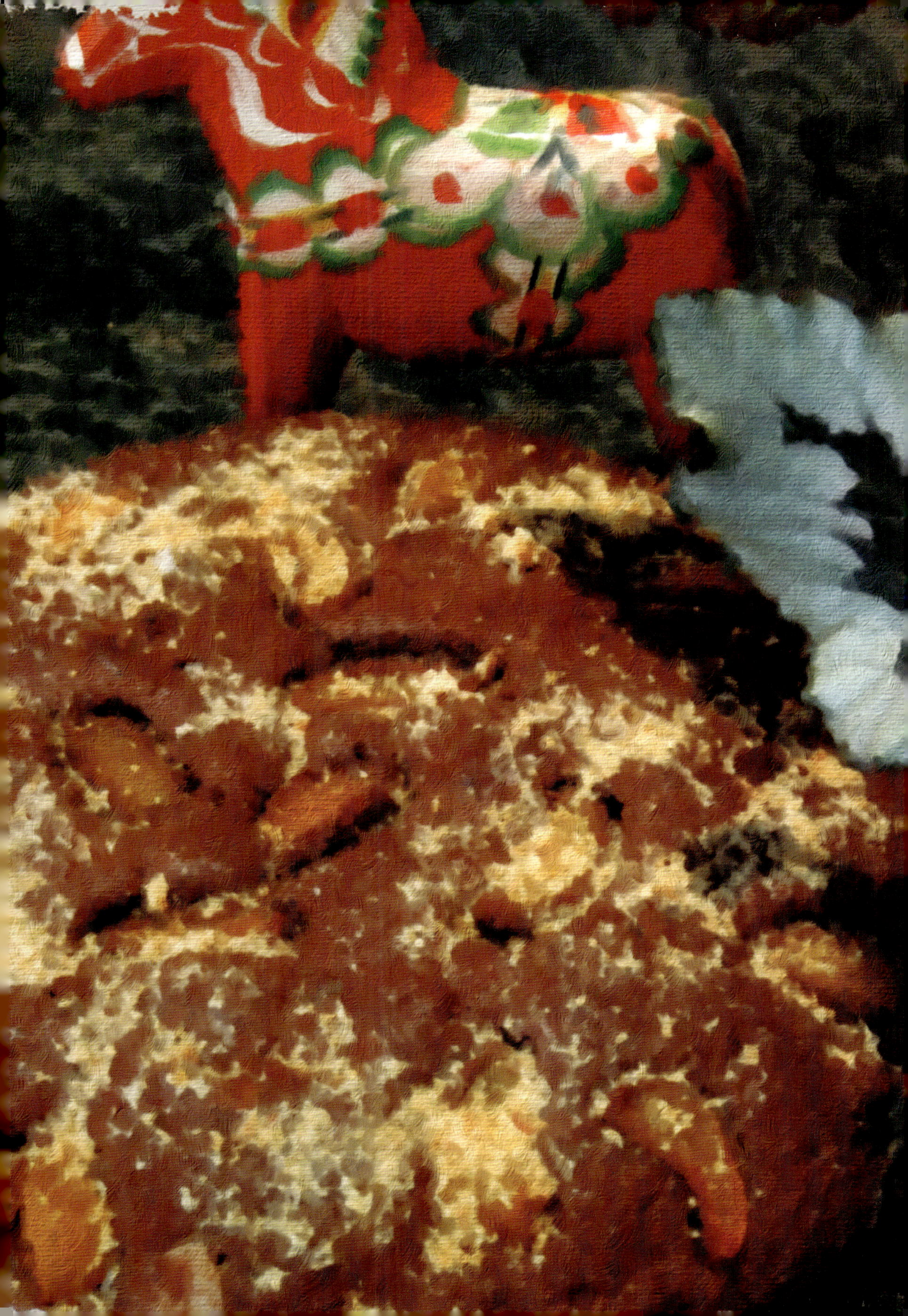

# Pear & Hazelnut Crumble Cake

*A little long winded to prepare, but a great favourite in the patisserie at teatime, and well worth the effort.*

175g soft brown sugar
175g butter
3 eggs
85g ground roast hazelnuts
100g self-raising flour
3 large poached pears
50g Belgian chocolate chips
½ tsp of cinnamon

For the crumble topping:
100g plain flour
40g butter
2 tbsp demarera sugar

Grease and line a 24cm deep cake tin.

Roast whole hazelnuts in the oven and rub them in a tea towel to remove the skins which are a little bitter. I prepare a large amount, blitz them in the processor and then keep them in a jar.

Cream butter and sugar together and add the eggs one by one alternately with the flour, and hazelnuts, sprinkling in the cinnamon at the last. Spread this mixture evenly in the tin, and chop the pears into ½" chunks, placing them evenly over the cake mix. Tinned pears are equally successful in this cake, if poaching fresh seems rather lengthy.

Sprinkle the chocolate chips over the pears.

Rub the butter into the flour with light finger tips for the crumble, add the sugar and spread evenly over the pears.

Bake in the centre of a moderate oven until you are sure the cake is firm in the middle, this can take 45–50 minutes depending on the oven.

# Spice Cake with Orange Jam

*Based on a festive French recipe, this is such an unusual and spectacular cake, but really quite simple to prepare.*

200ml milk
150g honey
125g butter
125g soft brown sugar
½ tsp ground ginger
a pinch each of ground cloves, anis, coriander and salt
¼ tsp cinnamon
275g self-raising flour
25g ground almonds
2 eggs
50g icing sugar

For the orange jam:
3 oranges
50g white sugar
1 leaf of gelatine

In a saucepan mix the honey, butter, sugar spices and salt and warm through until melted together. Take off the heat, cover and leave to infuse the flavours. Whisk the eggs in the milk and add to the melted mix. Stir in the flour and almonds making sure there are no pockets of flour in the mix. Butter and line a 25cm tin and bake for 40 minutes in a moderate oven.

**For the jam:** Peel 2 of the oranges and cut into sections with a sharp knife, between the membranes. Melt the sugar in 2tbsp water and cook quickly to make a syrup. Dissolve the gelatine in the juice of the remaining orange warming it in the microwave a little, and mix into the sugar syrup. Finally add the orange pieces cook for another 3 minutes and leave to cool.

**For the icing:** Heat 3tbsp water and add the icing sugar mixing well, spread onto the cake placing the orange jam in the centre.

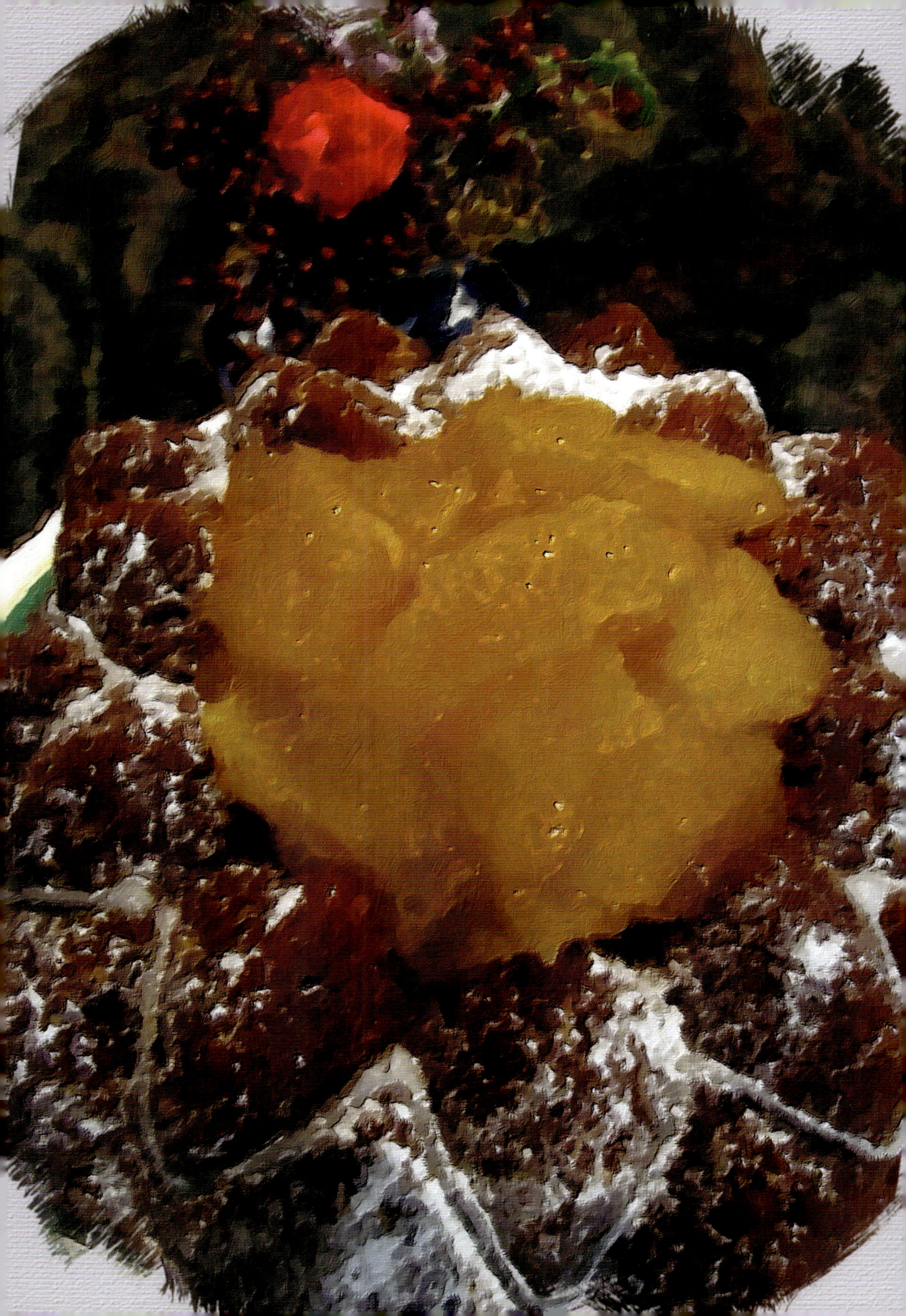

# Coffee Walnut Cake with Mocha Butter Cream

*When Autumn arrives along with sack of walnuts freshly gathered in Pau with the scent of the mountains trapped in the bag, this old favourite slides back on the shelf at Le Vieux Four. Embellished with freshly made espresso, available now to all but a few, a little sticky caramel and melted best dark chocolate added to the butter cream to perfect the flavours of a combination coffee experience, 'noisette, caramel and mocha all in one bite'!*

250g butter
250g self-raising flour
250g caster sugar
1 tbsp of espresso
4 eggs
50g chopped walnuts (optional)

For the filling:
130g icing sugar
130g butter
2 tsp espresso
50g melted dark chocolate

For the icing:
150g icing sugar
1 tbsp (approx) espresso
80g caster sugar for the caramel
walnuts to decorate

Grease 2 non stick sandwich tins, placing a piece of bake well paper in the centre of each to prevent the centre of this moist sponge from sticking.

Mix all the ingredients for the cake itself together thoroughly and bake in a moderate oven until risen and firm to the touch. Turn out and cool completely.

Mix the butter filling adding the cooled melted chocolate last and chill stirring well. Evenly join the cake halves with the butter icing.

Add the espresso to the icing sugar and mix to a spreadable consistency adding a little more sugar or coffee cautiously as needed, the icing must not run off the cake!

Melt the sugar over a low heat until it turns to a golden caramel, taking care not to burn the result which is quickly attained. Drizzle the golden liquid over the finished sponge and decorate with walnuts.

*Speciality Cakes*

# Whisky-Rich Fruit Cake with Walnut Brittle

*Sometimes the best recipes have evolved from a customer asking me to make something that does not end up quite what they had in mind, but at the end of the day is infinitely better and thankfully a huge success! This recipe happened exactly like that and everyone else seems to like it too and so it has found a permanent place next to the Dundee cakes in the shop.*

**275g currants**
**225g sultanas**
**60g peel**
**60g glacé cherries**
**1 tbsp whisky**
**225g flour**
**225g butter**

**225g dark brown sugar**
**4 eggs**
**1 tbsp black treacle**
**grated lemon zest**
**¼ tsp freshly grated nutmeg**
**¼ tsp cinnamon**

**For the walnut brittle:**
**2 tbsp caster sugar**
**50g walnut pieces**

Grease and line a 10" cake tin. Soak the dried fruits overnight with the whisky and spices.

Cream butter and sugar until a smooth cream and add the eggs alternately with the flour. Add all the fruit, the zests and treacle and mix thoroughly. Spoon into the tin and bake in a slow oven, my gas oven has a star setting, the lowest possible and I set it on the shelf below the middle. The cake is ready when risen slightly, firm to the touch and an appetising brown, taking 2½ to 3 hours in my oven.

Make a caramel by melting the sugar in a heavy bottomed saucepan, letting it take colour to a golden brown but not allowing it to burn. Mix in the walnut pieces and turn onto baking parchment to cool. The brittle can be chopped into small pieces when cold. Allow the cake to cool completely, brush lightly with apricot jam and sprinkle with the brittle.

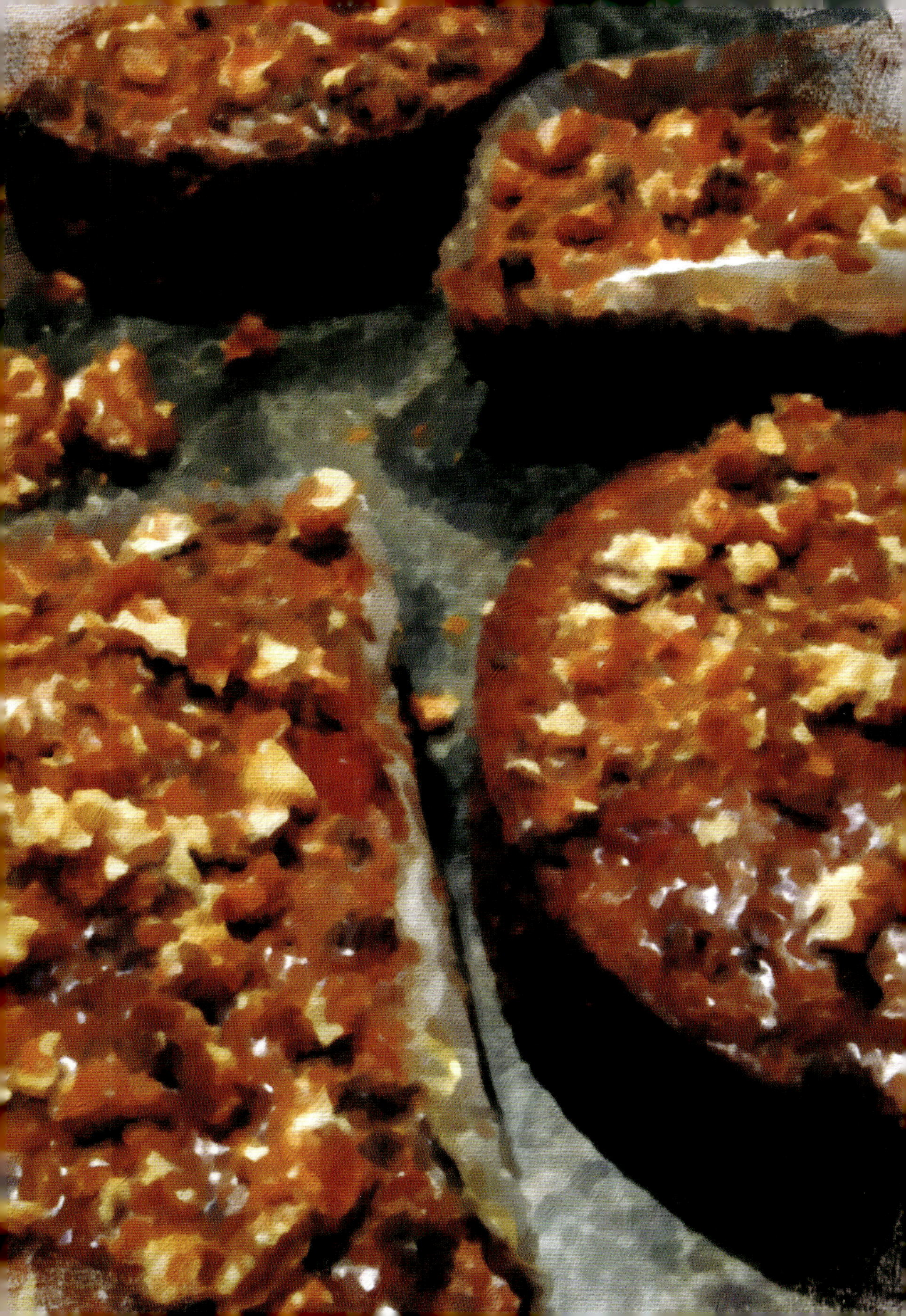

# Lavender & Almond Lemon Drizzle

*This is a variation of a recipe in my first book which I tried nervously, uncertain of the flavour combination, but it makes a wonderful summer cake.*

200g butter
200g sugar
4 eggs
100g self-raising flour
100g almonds
zest of 1 lemon
1 tsp dried lavender

For the drizzle:
3 tbsp icing sugar
juice of 2 lemons
2 tbsp water
1 tsp dried lavender

Cream the butter and sugar and add the eggs alternately with the dry ingredients. Finally add the zest and lavender. Bake in a moderate oven for 40 minutes until risen and golden brown.

Dissolve the icing sugar in the water and lemon juice over a low heat and then allow to boil until reduced and syrupy.

Add the lavender and having made holes with a cake tester pour the drizzle over the warm cake and serve.

# Caribbean Cake

*All the best flavours of the spice islands wrapped up in one cake! Just a sniff of it makes me long to go back there, and I know I am very lucky to have spent such happy times sailing the luscious blue waters of The Windward Islands.*

1 large ripe banana
½ small ripe papaya
1 lime
orange zest
1 tbsp Mount Gay rum
½ tsp grated nutmeg
½ tsp cinnamon
200g butter
200g soft light brown sugar
3 eggs
200g self-raising flour
50g plain flour

For the icing:
150g icing sugar
the juice and remaining lime zest

Line a 10" cake tin.

Cream butter and sugar until soft and creamy and add the eggs alternately with the flour mixed with the spices, and a little grated lime and orange zest. Mash the banana and chop the peeled and seeded papaya into small cubes. Add the fruit and rum to the cake mix folding in quickly so as not to mash the papaya pieces. Spread the mix in the tin and bake in a moderate oven until risen, brown and firm to the touch. Cool.

Mix the icing sugar with the juice of the lime and the rest of the grated zest and spread evenly over the cake.

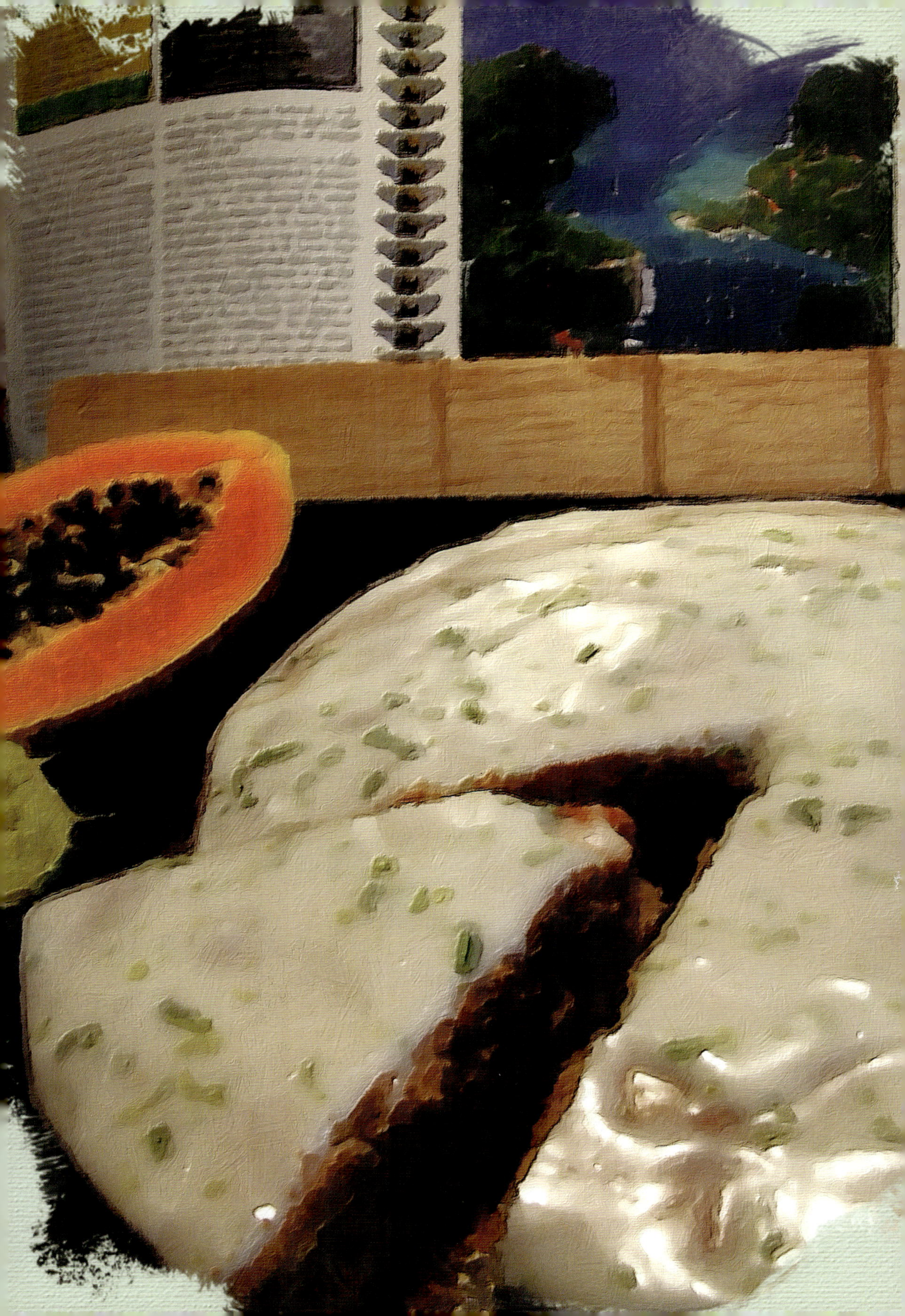

FRESH FR

## TY CAKES

*Fig Cake, with Honey & Orange*

*Plum Cake, with Almonds & Kirsch*

*Blood Orange & Rhubarb Loaf*

*Summer Fruit Mini Loaves*

*Black & White Pineapple Cake*

*Lemon Cake with Fresh Rhubarb Compote*

*Apple Strudel*

*Fresh Raspberry & Marzipan Towers*

*Roast Apricot Dacquoise with Vanilla Rice*

*Savarin with White Grapes & Kirsch*

*Soft Rum Cake with Crème Patissière & Cherry Coulis*

*Blackberry & Apple Cake with Almonds*

# Fig Cake with Honey & Orange

*Everyone in the town brings me their surplus fruit in the summer which is such a delight, whether I use it for jam or cakes, nothing is wasted. Last year was a glut year for the most wonderful figs, placed on my doorstep, hanging in bags on the front door, they were everywhere, so this cake was born in the autumn.*

200g butter
200g soft brown sugar
200g self-raising flour
4 large figs
1 tbsp clear honey
3 eggs
orange zest

Grease and line a 24cm cake tin.

Cream butter and sugar and add the eggs alternately with the flour. Stir in the honey and orange zest. Carefully peel the figs and roughly chop 3 for the cake mix, slicing the last one neatly for the top of the cake. Mix in the chopped figs allowing them to be well blended, as this adds to the texture of the finished cake.

Bake in the centre of a moderate oven and when it is risen and set, arrange the slices of reserved fig on the top and replace in the oven until the cake is cooked right through, and pleasingly brown on top.

Served warm with something creamy, this cake makes a wonderful dessert.

# Plum Cake with Almonds & Kirsch

*I have recently planted a plum tree in my garden and I await my first plum with bated breath. It did have a couple of flowers so I am ever hopeful, as it is now two years old. The pleasure of growing things and turning them into cakes and jams has become my new obsession.*

**200g caster sugar**
**200g butter**
**150g ground almonds**
**150g self-raising flour**
**3 eggs**
**6 ripe plums**
**25g flaked almonds**
**1 tbsp kirsch**

Grease and line a 24cm cake tin.

Cream butter and sugar and add the eggs alternately with the flour and ground almonds. Roughly chop 5 plums reserving the last to thinly slice for decoration. Stir in the plums and finally the kirsch. Spread the mixture in the tin and scatter the flaked almonds on the top arranging the slices of plum around the edge.

Bake in the centre of a moderate oven until well risen and firm to the touch.

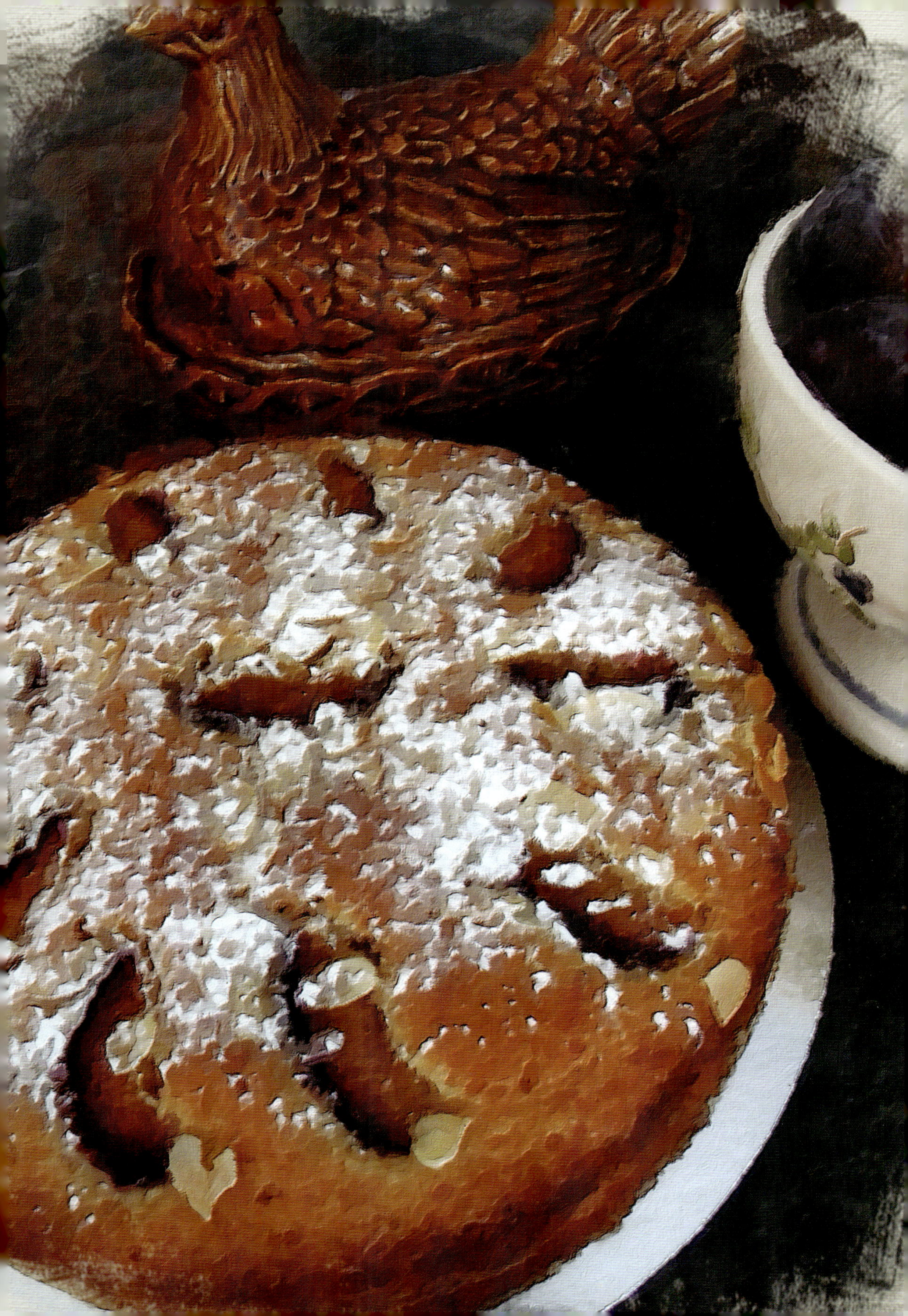

# Blood Orange & Rhubarb Loaf

Blood oranges and the first wonderful tender red rhubarb stalks appear in my local vegetable shop at the same time, tempting me to mix them together and make a cake. Best eaten very fresh, this loaf is wonderfully moist without being soggy and the tangy flavours compliment each other.

200g butter
200g caster sugar
200g self-raising flour
1 blood orange
2 tbsp roasted rhubarb
2 heaped tbsp of icing sugar

Place 250g chopped rhubarb in an oven dish with a tablespoon of sugar and bake until soft. By cooking the fruit this way, you will obtain a fairly dry purée for the cake.

Grease and line a loaf tin.

Cream butter and sugar and add the eggs alternately with the flour and the zest of the orange. Fold in 2 tbsp of the rhubarb using a slotted spoon to leave most of the juice behind.

Bake the loaf in a moderate oven until risen and firm especially in the middle.

While the cake is baking make a glacé icing with the icing sugar and blood orange juice, mixing just to a spreading consistency.

Ice when the cake has cooled and serve with whipped cream with the addition of the remaining roasted rhubarb and juice.

# Summer Fruit Mini Loaves

*Delicious little cakes that turn out almost like a cross between a doughnut and a cake with the taste of summer hidden inside.*

**For the filling:**
**200g summer fruits, blackcurrants, raspberries, and blueberries**
**1 large bramley apple, peeled and chopped**
**2 tbsp sugar**
**lemon juice to taste**

Melt the sugar with the fruit and boil for 10 mins as you would for jam, to make a thick purée when cooled.

**For the batter:**
**170g butter**
**200g caster sugar**
**3 eggs**
**300g self-raising flour**
**150g plain yogurt**

Grease and line a mini loaf tin bringing the baking parchment 1cm above the edge of each well to allow the loaves to rise evenly above the edge of the tin.

Blend the yogurt and eggs together and stir in the melted cooled butter.

Mix the dry ingredients with a pinch of salt and stir in the liquid mixture, whisking well to make a smooth batter. Carefully half fill each small tin and place a large teaspoon of the jam, before filling up equally until all the batter is used.

Bake in a moderate oven until golden, cooling in the tin before turning out and sprinkling with caster or icing sugar.

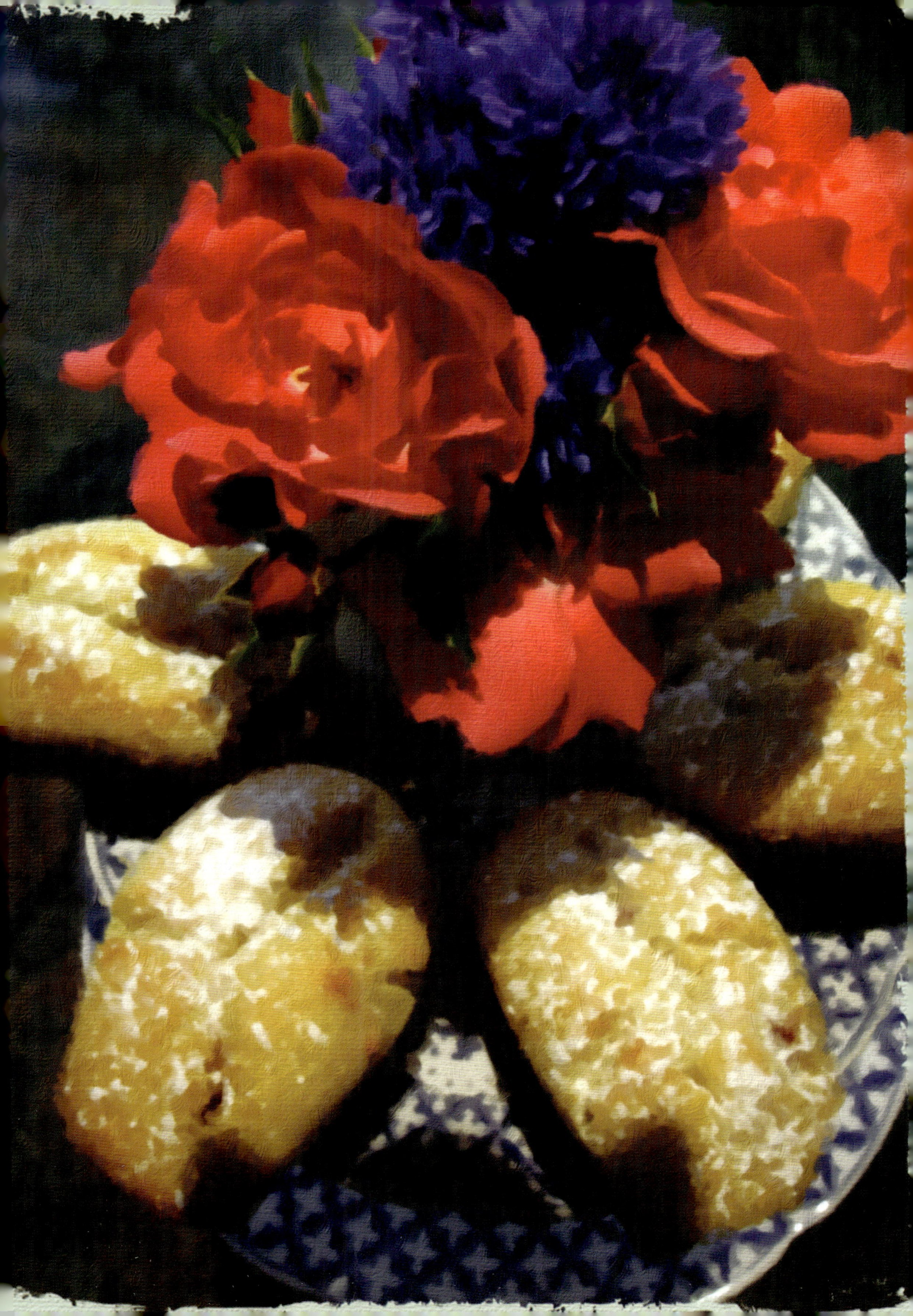

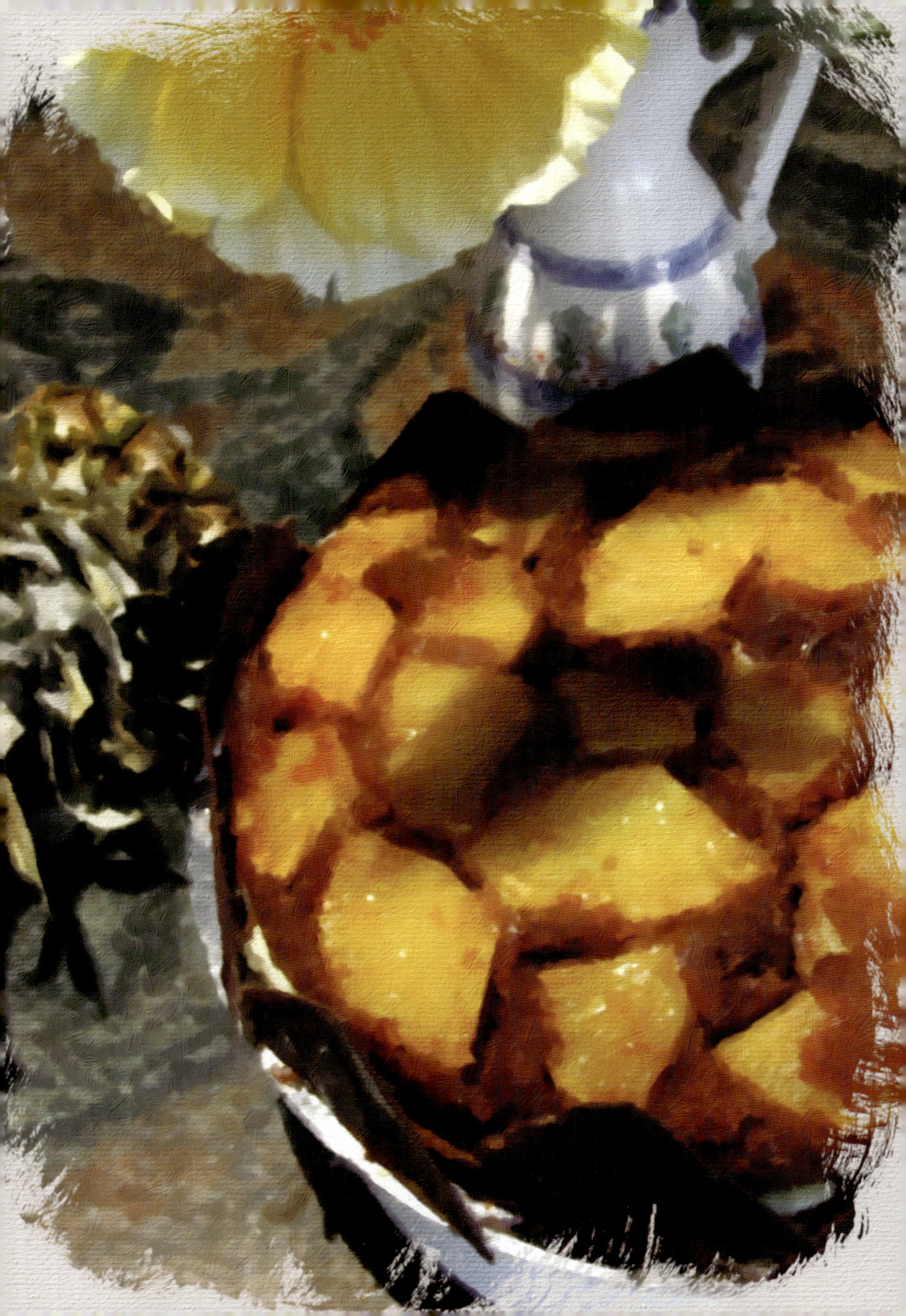

# Black & White Pineapple Cake

*This cake may seem a little laborious but is well worth the effort to produce a spectacular version of an upside down fresh pineapple cake.*

200g butter
½ large pineapple
330g caster sugar
200g self-raising flour
30g cocoa powder
4 eggs
150g dark Belgian chocolate
50ml pineapple juice

For the white chocolate ganache:
180g white chocolate
200ml double cream

Cut off the skin of the pineapple and cut in half lengthways. Cut into long slices about 5mm thick removing the hard central core. Line a loose based, 24cm non stick cake around the edge but not the base. In a small pan heat 130g of the sugar until a pale caramel is made and pour this into the base of the tin. Lay the slices of fruit evenly in the mould.

Mix the flour with the remaining sugar and the cocoa powder, and making a well in the centre add the eggs and melted butter. Mix well and spread in the tin covering the pineapple. Bake in a moderate oven until risen and firm to the touch.

While the cake is baking prepare the white ganache by softening the chocolate over hot water and adding 50ml of the liquid cream that has been heated to boiling point. Allow to cool and whisk in the remaining cream.

Carefully turn out the cake and allow to cool.

Melt the dark chocolate in a double boiler and spread quite thinly onto baking parchment. As it hardens cut into squares to decorate the edge of the cake. Cut in half and drizzle the bottom layer with pineapple juice keeping some juice for the top.

Spread the white chocolate ganache onto the base of the cake saving a tablespoonful. Place the top layer on the filling and decorate the cake around the edge by attaching the dark chocolate squares with the white ganache. Drizzle the finished cake with the remaining juice and chill.

# Lemon Cake with Fresh Rhubarb Compote

*I have a loose bottomed ring mould cake tin in my cupboard that is not suitable for many cakes, but is perfect for this one. With a decorative scalloped top and the hole through the centre filled with fresh fruit it looks spectacular, but I have learnt that the cake must be turned out quickly or the steam will cause it to attach itself firmly to the tin and this is a complete disaster in my quest for perfect presentation.*

For the compote:
200g rhubarb
80g sugar
Juice of ½ a lemon

For the cake:
200g butter
3 eggs
200g caster sugar
200g self-raising flour
Zest of 1 lemon, blanched and finely chopped
Juice of ½ a lemon
150g fresh raspberries
20g icing sugar

Butter and flour a ring mould cake tin.

Melt the butter and set on one side.

Whisk the eggs with the sugar and lemon zest until white and doubled in volume. Fold in the sieved flour, followed by the melted butter and the lemon juice, carefully continuing to turn the mix until smooth. Bake in the centre of a moderate oven until risen and firm.

While the cake is baking prepare the rhubarb. Remove the tough outer strings with a peeler and cut into 5cm lengths.

In a small heavy pan warm the sugar with a tablespoon of water to make a light caramel, add the rhubarb and lemon juice, cover and cook over a gentle heat for 10 minutes. Keep a few pieces of rhubarb that still hold their shape to decorate the cake.

As soon as the mould comes out of the oven turn the cake out onto a cooling rack, as if it is allowed to cool in the tin it may stick.

Cut the cake carefully in half and spread the lower half with the compote before replacing the top. Fill the centre with fresh raspberries and rhubarb pieces and sprinkle with icing sugar. A little piped lemon glacé makes a tasty attractive addition.

*Fresh Fruity Cakes*

# An Apple Streudel

*A German recipe, this is the best one I have ever found for a simple streudle. Apples are never in short supply from my bramley tree in the autumn, probably about 60 or 70 years old. I cannot decide whether I like it best in spring covered in beautiful prolific blossom, or in September when I struggle to process and not waste the abundance of the huge green apples that it bears year after year.*

**270g flour**
**1 egg yolk**
**pinch of salt**
**4 tbsp of sunflower oil**
**10g butter**

**For the filling:**
**1.5kg of bramley apples**
**100g raisins**
**3 tbsp caster sugar**
**pinch of cinnamon**
**4 tbsp breadcrumbs**

Mix the flour with the egg yolk, salt, oil and 75ml water to make an elastic dough. Gather into a ball and chill for a couple of hours.

Meanwhile prepare the apples. Peel and chop the apples into quarters and then into eighths.

Roll out the pastry as thinly as possible on a tea towel. Spread evenly with the filling ingredients and by holding the ends of the tea towel, roll the strudel. Place on a lined baking tray, brush with melted butter, sprinkle with sugar and cook in a moderate oven for about 50 mins.

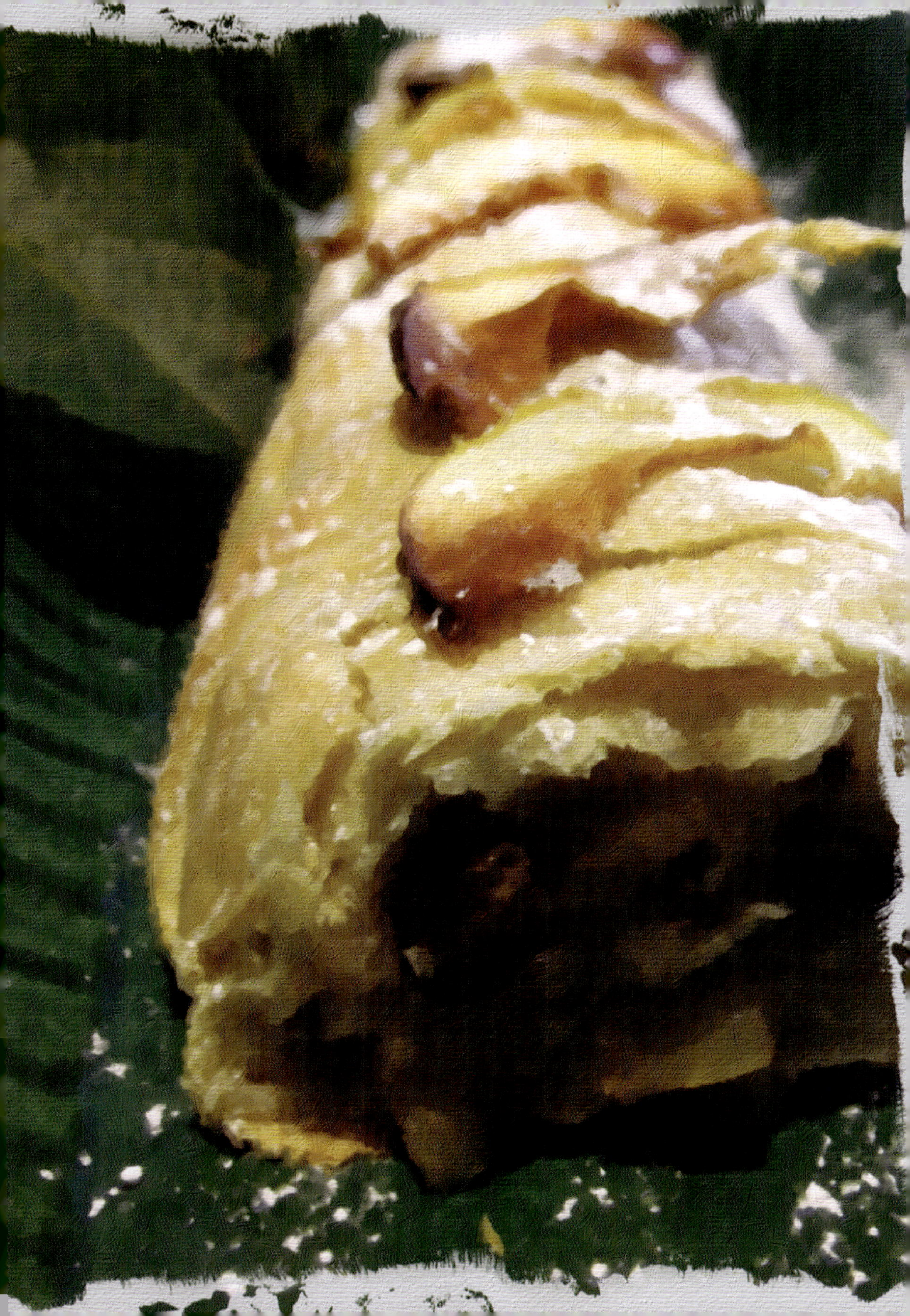

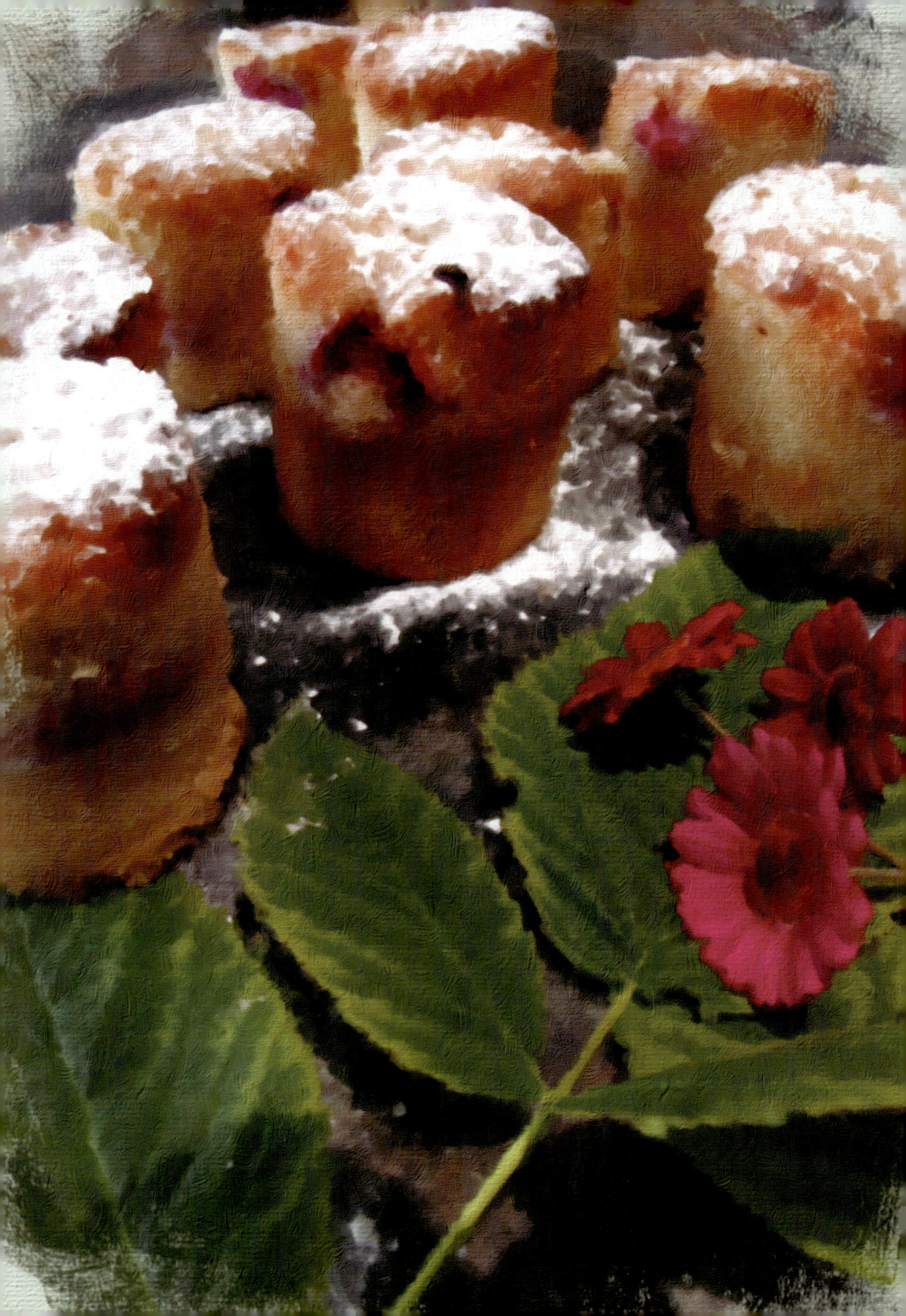

# Fresh Raspberry & Marzipan Towers

*These little muffins were a mistake but turned out to be a favourite although they were not quite what I had in mind when I began to plan them. I bake them in baby sponge cake tins which turns them into small sort of towers, very unique, but actually they work very well as muffins and it involves a lot less washing up, and fiddling around with baking parchment when they are baked in a muffin case.*

**270g butter**
**3 eggs**
**270g caster sugar**
**120g self-raising flour**
**150g ground almonds**
**50g marzipan**
**fresh raspberries**

Cream the butter and sugar, and add the eggs alternately with the flour and ground almonds. Break the marzipan up into small pieces about the size of a hazelnut and stir into the cake mix. Three-quarters fill the muffin cases and place a couple of raspberries on the top of each one. Bake in the centre of a moderate oven until firm to the touch, keeping a close eye so they are not burnt on top.

Warm with cream… just perfect.

# Roast Apricot Dacquoise with Vanilla Rice

*Roasting apricots really brings out their flavour, and on this base of almond meringue cake and creamy vanilla rice, they are sublime.*

3 egg whites
130g caster sugar
80g ground almonds
50g icing sugar
1 tbsp flaked almonds
20g butter
350g fresh apricots
apricot jam to glaze

For the vanilla rice:
60g round pudding rice
250ml milk
½ tsp vanilla essence
1 egg yolk

Whisk the egg whites until firm peaks adding 80g of caster sugar towards the end. Fold in the ground almonds and 40g of the icing sugar. Draw a 24cm circle on baking parchment, and with the aid of a piping bag make a crown around the edge of the circle and pipe a spiral to fill in the centre. Bake in a moderate oven for 15 minutes.

To prepare the rice, plunge into boiling water and strain when a reboil is reached. Place the rice in a pan with the milk and vanilla and cook very slowly until the milk is adsorbed. Off the heat add the egg yolk and mix well, leaving the rice to cool.

Take the dacquoise from the oven and allow to cool, it should be soft in the middle.

Melt the butter and turn the oven up to fairly hot. Cut and destone the apricots laying them on a baking tray, brush them with the melted butter, sprinkle with the rest of the sugar and put them in the oven for 10 minutes until they take a little colour.

Spread the rice on the dacquoise, arrange the apricots in a rosette shape and glaze with the warm, sieved apricot jam. Best eaten as soon as possible after preparation.

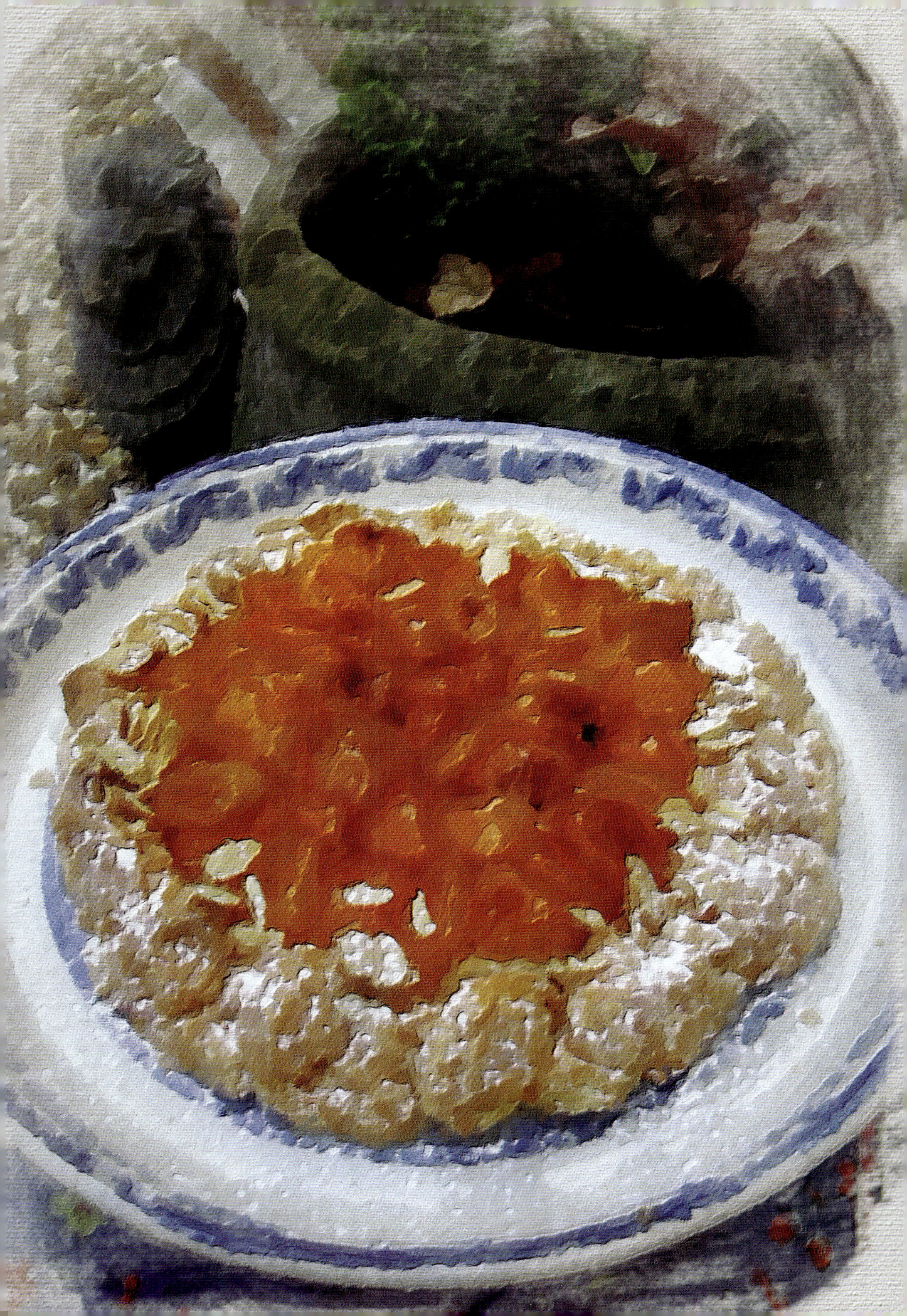

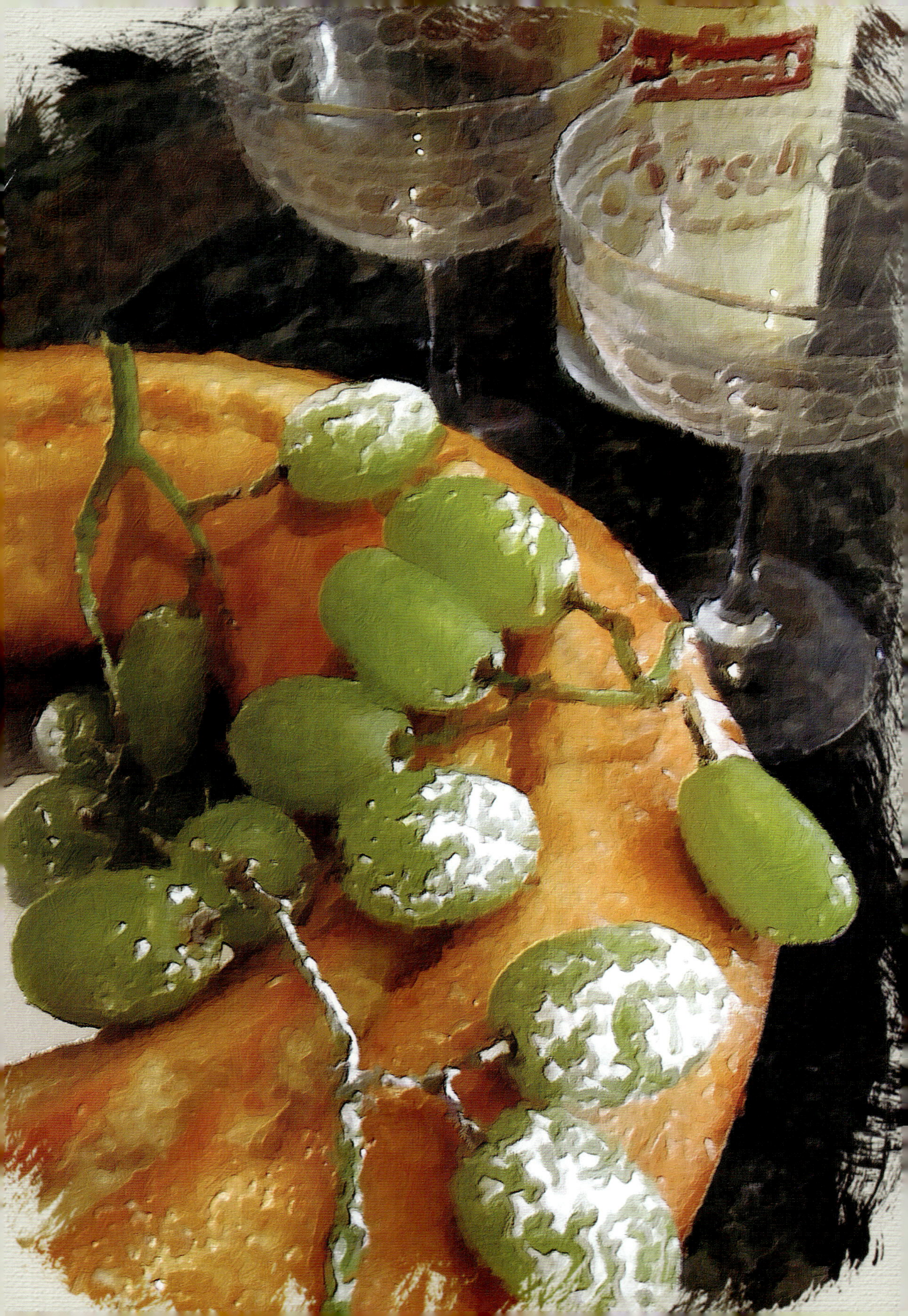

# Savarin with White Grapes & Kirsch

*A traditional old French recipe, not unlike a rum baba, for a keen cook who wants to try something a little different, but who can feel very proud when it is done and on the table.*

**1 sachet of dried easy bake yeast**
**150ml milk**
**300g flour**
**½ tsp salt**
**130g soft butter**
**500g white seedless, sweet grapes**
**150g sugar**
**1 tbsp kirsch**
**3 eggs**

**For the syrup:**
**400g caster sugar**
**1 tbsp kirsch**
**75ml water**

In a bowl mix together all the dry ingredients, not forgetting the yeast, and making a well in the centre add the eggs and the milk warmed a little to encourage the yeast. Mix well to form a dough and then add the butter in small pieces until it is all mixed in. Knead well, lifting and turning until it becomes a little less sticky.

Butter a 26cm savarin mould and press in the dough, leaving it to rise until double in size at room temperature.

Bake in a hot oven for 20–30 minutes until light and golden brown. Turn out of the tin on to a cooling rack.

Make the syrup with the water and sugar, boiling it for 5 minutes. Add the kirsch, and spoon carefully and evenly over the warm savarin.

Marinate the grapes in a little sugar and kirsch in the fridge and fill the centre of the cake to serve.

# Soft Rum Cake with Creme Patissiere & Cherry Coulis

*An old recipe originating from Alsace, using the cracked cherry stones to give a faint almond flavour to the coulis, and with a method for the cake mix that gives a wonderful soft texture. Surround this cake with fresh cherries and serve warm or cold with a glass of white wine from the same region, they compliment each other perfectly.*

250g soft butter
200g caster sugar
300g self-raising flour
1 egg and 2 yolks
2 tbsp Mount Gay golden rum
    (*this rum has the best flavour for me but you might choose another*)
a few drops of the finest vanilla essence
270g crème pâtissière flavoured with rum

For the cherry coulis:
200g sugar
350g cherries

*Fresh Fruity Cakes*

Soften the butter in a bowl and add the sugar, flour, egg and yolks, rum and vanilla. Mix well and refrigerate for at least 1 hour.

Meanwhile prepare the cherry coulis. In a pan put 50ml of water, the sugar and the cherries still with their stones. Bring to the boil and then press through a sieve, crushing the fruit. Take a few stones, crack them and wrap in a small muslin bag, leaving this in the coulis to impart a flavour of almonds.

Grease and line a 24cm loose bottomed cake mould.

Separate the doughy cake mix into 2 portions, ¼ and ¾ spreading the larger portion in the prepared tin. Spread with the crème and cover with the second layer of mix. Bake in a moderate oven for 30–40 minutes and serve with the coulis and plenty of fresh cherries.

# Blackberry & Apple Cake with Almonds

*Just the cake to whizz together after a long September walk in Dorset gathering blackberries!*

½ large bramley apple
75g blackberries
200g butter
200g caster sugar
85g ground almonds
125g self-raising flour
3 eggs

Grease and line a 24cm cake tin.

Cream butter and sugar and add eggs alternately with the flour and ground almonds. Peel and grate the apple and stir into the cake mix with the blackberries, (blackcurrants work equally well). Spread in the tin and bake in a moderate oven until golden and firm.

*Fresh Fruity Cakes*

# VEGETA

## *With all the following vegetable cakes the trick is*
## *and to steam*

# CAKES

...ry the cooked or grated flesh as much as possible,
...il prior to use

*Pumpkin Cake*

*Beetroot Cake with Ginger, Mascarpone Icing with Fresh Raspberries*

*Sweet Potato Cake*

*Courgette, Cocoa & Hazelnut Sponge*

*Spicy Squash Mini Loaves with Sunflower Kernels & Pumpkin Seeds*

*Fennel Cake, with Crème Patissière & Fresh Apricots*

# Pumpkin Cake

*An old French recipe from Limous, a sort of caramelised pumpkin flan, lovely served with stewed prunes or red plums. I made a damson coulis which made a good flavour combination and I found that microwaving the pumpkin works well and keeps it dry, placing it in the food processor to make a smooth purée.*

**1½ kg pumpkin giving about 800g of purée**
**175g sugar for the caramel**
**4 eggs**
**200g sugar**
**2 tbsp cornflour**
**½ tsp vanilla essence**
**pinch of salt**
**½ tsp ground ginger**

Peel the pumpkin, removing all the filaments and pips. Cut the flesh into cubes and steam for 3 minutes. Strain and mash to a fine purée.

In a pan melt the sugar in 2 tbs of water and boil to a light brown caramel. Tip the caramel into a flan dish and tip the dish to coat the base and sides.

Beat the eggs and mix with the pumpkin. Add the sugar, the essence and the flour, salt and ginger. Tip into the mould and standing in a bain-marie, cook in a moderate oven for 45 minutes until browned and set.

Make a coulis with stewed damsons or plums to accompany the flan.

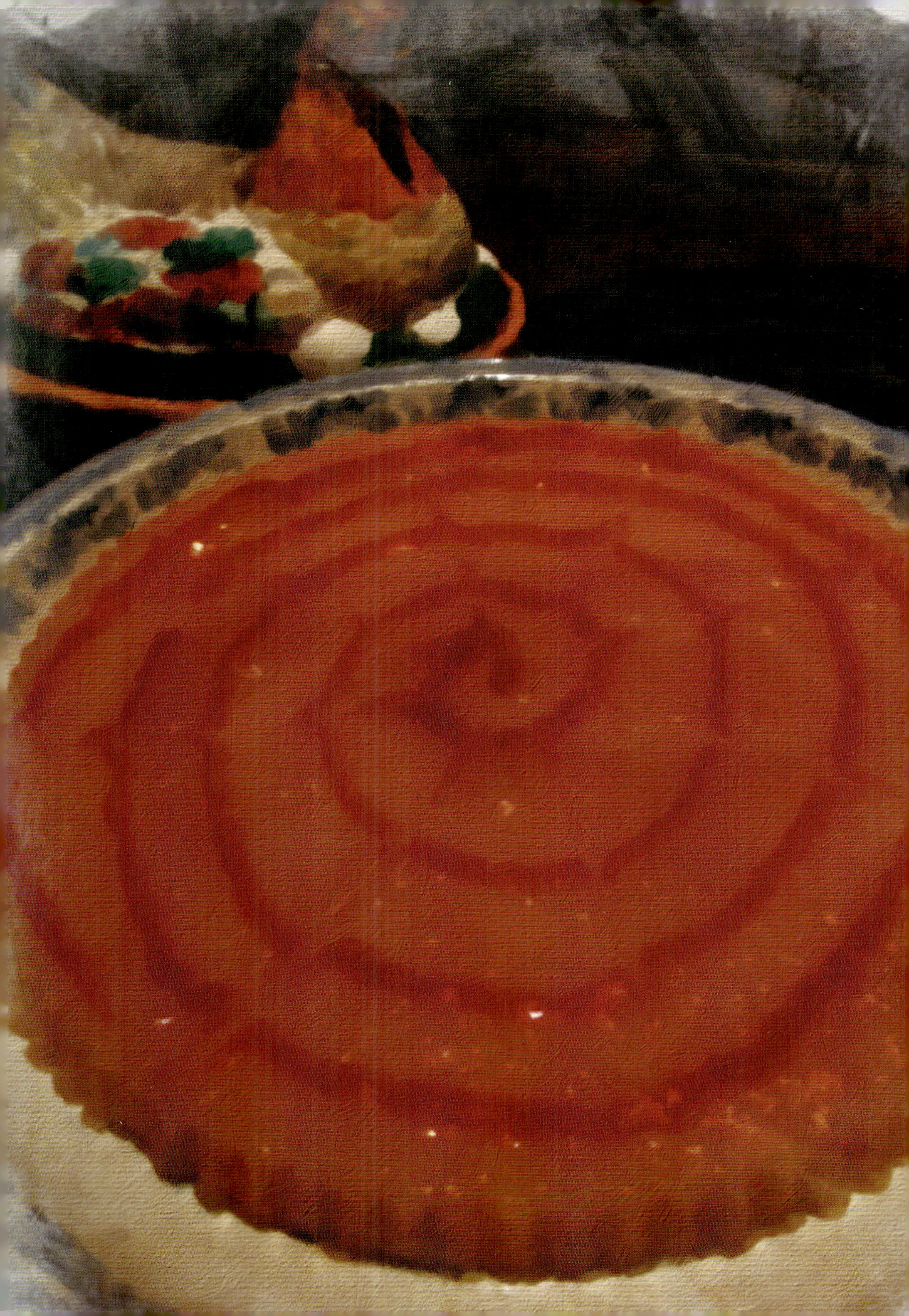

# Beetroot Loaf with Ginger, Mascarpone Icing with Fresh Raspberries

*It feels like cheating to eat a couple of one's five a day like this, or should it be seven now we are told to keep us really healthy.*

250g raw beetroot, peeled and finely grated
125g butter
125g golden syrup
125g soft dark brown sugar
3 eggs separated
2 tbsp natural yogurt
300g self-raising flour
½ tsp grated fresh nutmeg
½ tsp cinnamon
1 tsp grated fresh ginger

For the icing:
100g icing sugar
400g mascarpone
100g fresh raspberries

**Grease and line 2 loaf tins.**

In a heavy saucepan melt together the butter, sugar and syrup. Squeeze the beetroot in paper towel to remove excess moisture and add this and the eggs whisked all together with the yogurt off the heat until smoothly blended. Add the ginger and spices, followed by the flour making sure it is thoroughly mixed in with no lumps. Bake in a moderate oven until risen and firm. Cool on a rack.

Mix the mascarpone and icing sugar and decorate with fresh raspberries, the topping will turn a shade of pink on contact with the cake but this adds to the charm!

*Vegetable Cakes*

# Sweet Potato Cake

*In the West Indies it is almost all they have got so they are bound to have made cake out of it, aren't they?*

*With a rich butter icing with a kick of lime, it does have a certain appeal and is surely unusual for a teatime treat.*

800g sweet potatoes
juice of 1 lime
pinch of salt
3 eggs
150g sugar
150g self-raising flour
230g soft butter
½ tsp cinnamon
1 tsp vanilla essence
4 tbsp Mount Gay rum

For the icing:
150g icing sugar
150g butter
zest and juice of 1 lime
a little grated nutmeg

Wash and peel the sweet potatoes. Cut into pieces and soak in water for 10 minutes with the juice of one lime added. Cook for 20 minutes in boiling salted water.

Mash the vegetable to a smooth purèe and incorporate the eggs, followed by the sugar and butter. Whisk briskly and add the rest of the flavourings.

Pour into a buttered cake mould and bake in a moderate oven until golden brown making sure a knife dipped into the centre comes out clean.

Mix the icing ingredients using the nutmeg to sprinkle on the iced cake.

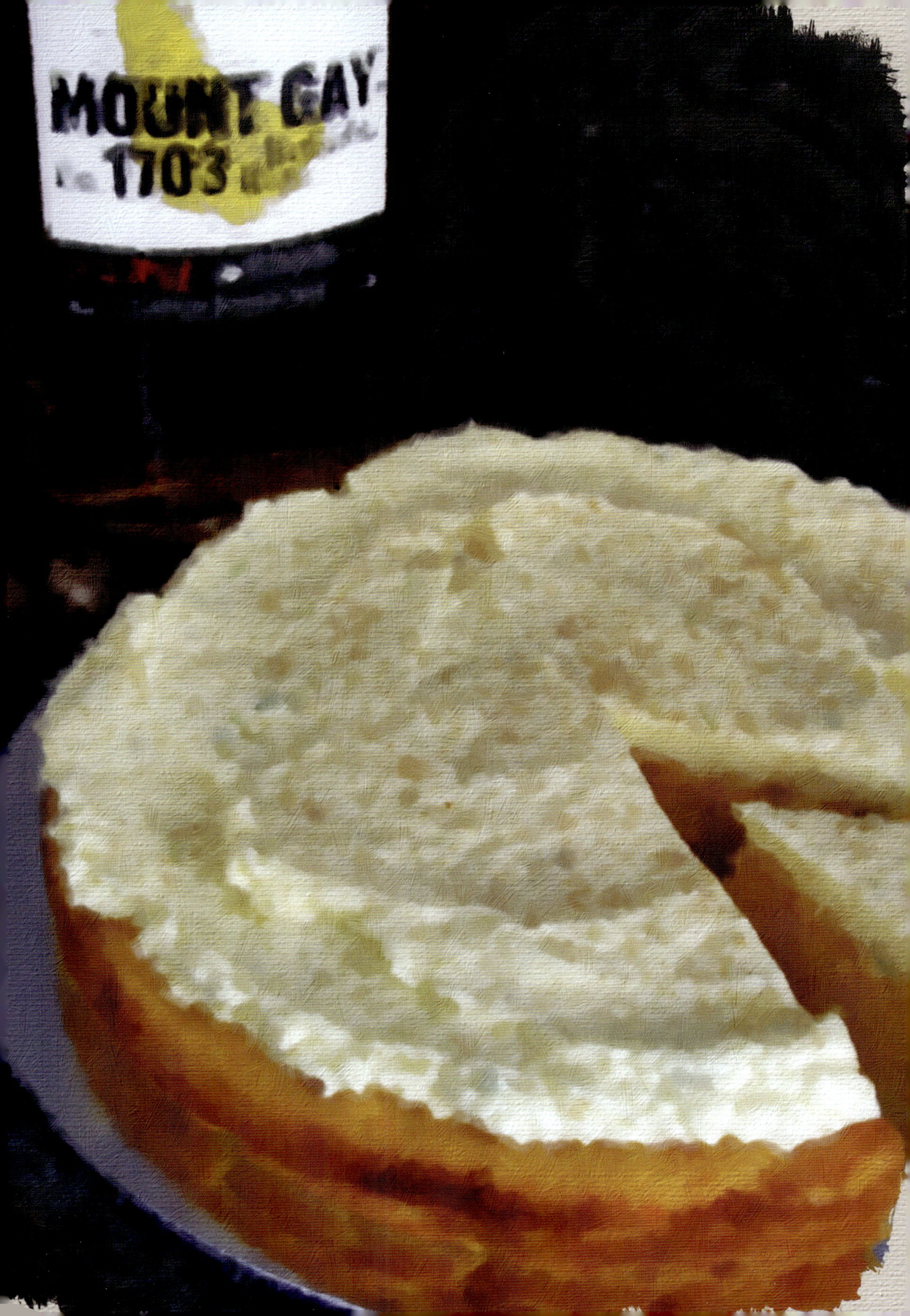
MOUNT GAY
1703

# Courgette, Chocolate & Hazelnut Sponge Cake

*Not unlike the West Indian glut of sweet potato, I always seem to have an abundance of courgettes from my garden in the summer and so had to devise a cake recipe to use them.*

60g roasted skinned hazelnuts processed
    to a fine crumb
3 eggs
180g soft brown sugar
200g peeled courgettes, grated
130g self-raising flour
pinch of salt
60g cocoa powder
a few drops of vanilla essence
2 tbsp sunflower oil
200g chocolate butter icing
roughly chopped hazelnuts and
    chocolate shavings to decorate

Finely grate the courgettes and squeeze in a cloth or absorbent paper to remove some of the moisture.

Whisk eggs and sugar until light and beat in the courgette, ground hazelnuts, oil and vanilla. Fold in the flour, cocoa and salt, and spread between 2 greased sandwich tins. Bake until risen and firm in a moderate oven. Turn onto a cooling rack and ice when cold.

Blueberries add a delicious summer touch to this cake.

Sweetened cream cheese makes a good alternative to chocolate butter icing.

# Spicy Squash Mini Loaves with Sunflower Kernels & Pumpkin Seeds

*This cake sounds much too healthy for one of my creations but I have developed a taste for seeds lately and find them, like nuts, flavourful and of course nutritious for my vegetable cake recipes.*

250g peeled, grated butternut squash, squeezed in a tea towel to remove excess moisture
150g soft butter
150g soft light brown sugar
300g self-raising flour
2 eggs
1 tsp each of ground ginger, cinnamon & nutmeg
2 tbsp sunflower oil
½ tsp salt

For the top:
2 tbsp each of pumpkin seeds & sunflower kernels
3 tbsp maple syrup

Line a tray of mini loaf tins with buttered baking parchment bringing it up 1cm higher than the edge of the tin.

Cream butter and sugar and stir in the oil and grated squash. Fold in the flour, salt and spices alternately with the beaten eggs. Fill the cases equally and bake in a moderate oven until well risen. Roast the seeds for 5 minutes or so and then mix them with the syrup making a sticky topping for each little cake.

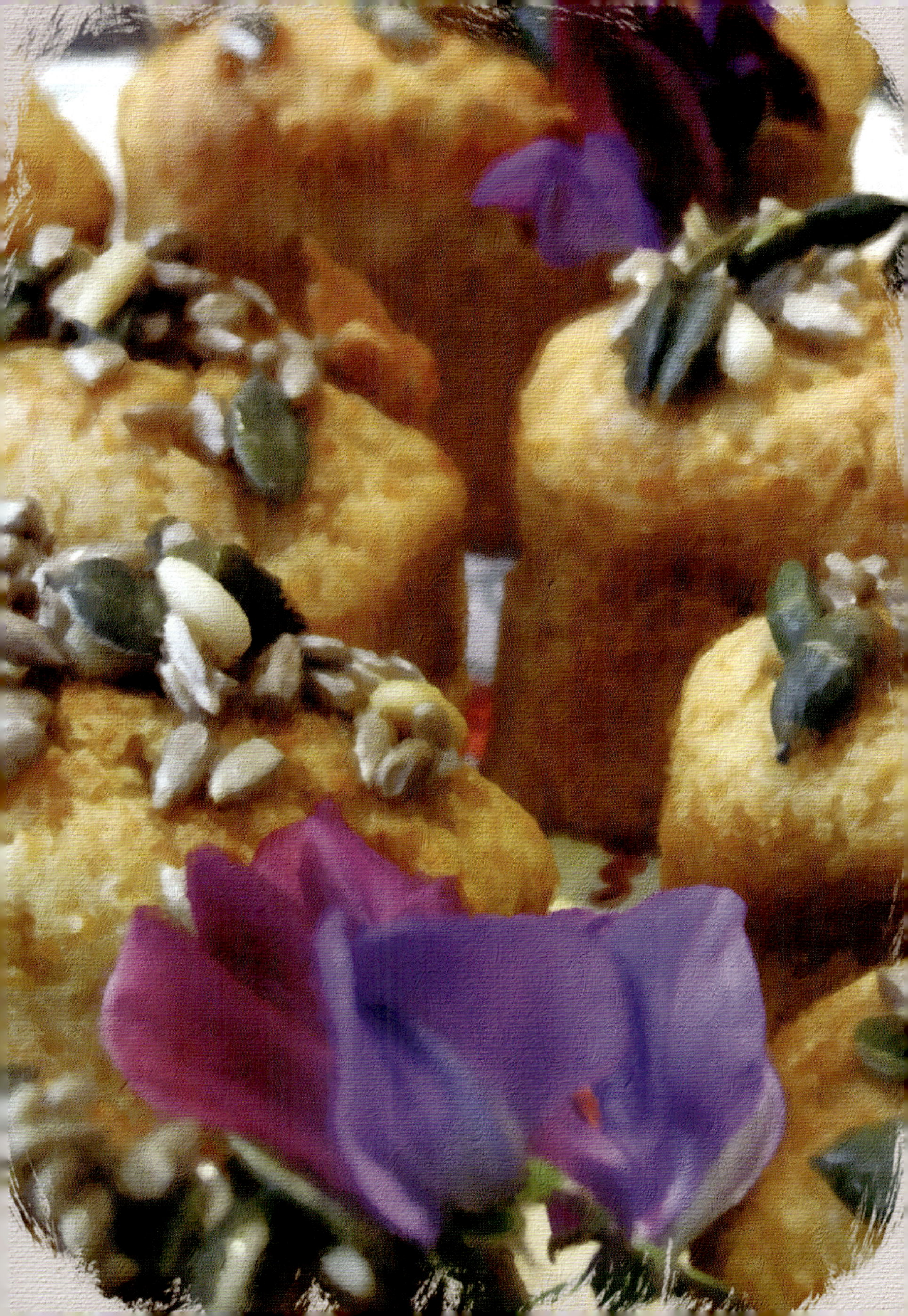

# Fennel Cake, with Crème Patissière & Fresh Apricots

*This cake is guaranteed to protect the house from the cruelest of sorcerer's spells.*

300g fennel
3 eggs
150g sugar
100g soft butter

150g flour
3 tbsp of crème patissière
5 ripe apricots

Discard any damaged outside layers, cut the fennel into pieces and steam for 10 minutes.

Separate the eggs and beat the yolks with half of the sugar until a white cream. Work in the butter and then the flour. Purée the fennel and stir into the mixture. Whisk the whites and progressively add the rest of the sugar. Fold into the rest. Spread into a buttered 24cm tin and bake in a moderately hot oven for 35 minutes until brown.

Serve cooled, spread with the crème and the apricots quartered and placed in circles.

*Vegetable Cakes* 59

## OLD FASHIONE

# FRENCH CAKES

*Biscuit de Savoie*

*Gateau Basque aux Cerises Noir*

*Fouace*

*Paris-Brest*

*Tropézienne*

*Pastis des Landes*

*Forêt Noire*

*Dacquoise aux Pistaches*

# Biscuit de Savoie

*This cake was created in the fourteenth century by the cook of the Count of Savoie, Amedée VI, in honour of the Emperor, Charles IV and would have been decorated with a figure representing the Count wearing a crown.*

4 eggs
100g icing sugar
a few drops of vanilla essence
50g flour

50g cornflour
25g butter
30g sugar crystals

Butter a brioche mould and dust lightly with cornflour.

Separate the eggs and mix the yolks with the sugar and vanilla until white and creamy. Stir in the two varieties of flour and mix well. Whisk the egg whites fairly stiff but not dry and fold them carefully and completely into the cake mix. Pile the mixture into the mould and bake in a moderate oven for 40 minutes.

Leave until cooled before turning onto a cooling rack, and sprinkling with sugar crystals.

The addition of grated orange or lemon adds flavour to this simple cake.

# Gateau Basque aux Cerises Noir

A traditional variation of my Gateau Basque that has remained such a favourite at *Le Vieux Four* over the last twenty years.

280g self-raising flour
1 egg plus 3 yolks
200g butter
200g sugar

30g ground almonds
pinch of salt
pot of black cherry jam

Place the flour in a bowl and add the egg plus 2 yolks, butter, sugar, almonds and salt. Work all together until a smooth, firm dough. Let this rest for an hour or so in the fridge. Butter a 25cm flan or a deep quiche mould works well and press ⅔ of the pastry in the base, forming a crust with your fingers around the edge. Fill the centre with jam and roll out the rest of the dough to cover. Pinch the edges together with a little cold water, brush with the remaining egg yolk beaten, and bake in moderately hot oven for 40 minutes.

You could, of course, make your own fresh black cherry purée, when they are in season.

# Fouace

*A gateau from the Middle Ages eaten on days of Fête or holidays, in certain regions of provincial France.*

500g flour
120ml milk
1 pkt of easy bake yeast
4 eggs
5 tsp orange flower water
190g caster sugar
320g butter

Mix the flour and yeast in a bowl and having warmed the milk a little add carefully to the flour. Add the eggs, one by one, the orange flower water and finally the sugar, combining all to a smooth dough.

Cut the butter into pieces and work in gradually and then leave the mix to rise for 1 hour at room temperature. Knead again and wrapping in cling film leave to rest in the fridge for 3 hours.

Shape into a crown on a baking tray and prove at room temperature for 1 hour. Sprinkle with sugar and bake at a moderate temperature for 30 minutes.

Serve when cool.

# Paris-Brest

*A French masterpiece, a cake both rustic and sublimely grand, not so hard to do if you follow the recipe carefully.*

100g of chopped, blanched almonds
30g butter
1 egg yolk
3 tbsp icing sugar

**For the choux pastry:**
60g butter
1 tsp sugar
pinch of salt
120g sieved flour
3 eggs

**For the butter cream:**
3 yolks
100g sugar
180g butter
200g powdered praline
250ml stiffly whipped cream

**To make the praline:** Melt 100g of caster sugar until it makes a golden caramel and add 100g of chopped, blanched and lightly roasted almonds. Stir until the nuts are coated in the caramel and then pile onto baking parchment to cool. When cold whiz in a food processor until a fine, breadcrumb like consistency is reached.

Roast the chopped almonds in a hot oven until golden. Cool.

**Prepare the choux pastry:** Add the butter to 200ml of water with the sugar and salt. Bring to the boil and take off the heat. Tip in the flour all at once and stir vigorously over the heat to dry the paste until it appears to form a ball leaving the sides of the pan. Add the eggs one by one off the heat mixing well. The mix should form soft peaks which fall over when raised with a wooden spoon.

Draw a circle on baking parchment on a tray and pipe the dough guided by your line. The width of the raw pastry should be about 15mm. Brush with egg yolk and sprinkle with the chopped almonds having lightly toasted them first.

Small individual versions of this cake can be piped in the same way.

Cook the choux in a moderately hot oven for 30–35 minutes until risen and golden brown allowing it to cool in the oven.

**To make the butter cream:** Work the butter until very soft and beat in the egg yolks, sugar and praline. Incorporate the cream folding until completely blended. Chill. Cut the choux carefully into two halves and pipe the butter cream generously into the lower half before replacing the top and sprinkling with icing sugar.

# Tropézienne

Anyone who has tasted this simple joy of confection in the place where it was born will want, if they like to cook at all, to have a go at recreating the wonderful soft, light gooeyness of this cake and dream themselves to be in St Tropez.

100ml milk
1 sachet of easy bake yeast
350g flour
70g soft butter
juice of ½ a lemon
1 egg
50g icing sugar
pinch of salt
2 tbsp caster sugar
2 tbsp of sugar crystals
    (I found these in Morrisons)

For the crème patissière:
350ml milk
a few drops of vanilla essence
60g sugar
4 egg yolks
30g flour
75ml whipped cream

Warm the milk and add the butter. In a bowl mix the yeast with the flour and salt, then making a well in the centre add the butter-milk mixture, the lemon juice, the egg and the icing sugar. Mix well to a brioche like consistency. Let rest at room temperature for 2 hours.

Rework the dough and form into a round galette about 1.5cm thick, finally placing it into a buttered 24cm cake tin. Brush with a little melted butter, sprinkle with caster sugar and leave for 1 hour.

Bake in a moderate oven for 20–25 minutes.

**Prepare the crème patissière:** Mix the sugar with the egg yolks until white and add the flour mixing well. Bring the milk to the boil and add it little by little to the egg mixture whisking all the time. Replace on the heat and stir until the custard thickens to a smooth cream. Add the vanilla essence and when cooled stir in the whipped cream. Place in the fridge stirring often to prevent a skin from forming.

Cool the cake and cut in half, sandwiching back together with the crème filling. Sprinkle with the crystallised sugar.

# Pastis des Landes

*In South-West France there are various cakes that carry the name Pastis but this one is the least complicated to make, some of them requiring a much higher level of expertise from the patissier.*

130g butter
5 eggs
200g sugar
3 tbsp rum
3 tbsp milk
1 tbsp orange flower water
1 tsp vanilla essence
1 sachet easy bake yeast
500g flour
1 tsp salt

Mix the flour with the dried yeast and the salt. In a bowl beat 4 eggs with the sugar until white and frothy, add the melted butter, rum, orange flower water and vanilla. Work the flour progressively in to the mixture until you have a firm dough. Sprinkle with flour and leave to prove at room temperature for 3 hours.

Work the dough thoroughly again and place in a buttered brioche mould. Prove for 2 hours more. Brush with beaten egg and cut a cross in the top with scissors. Bake in a moderately hot oven for 25 minutes.

I sometimes bake mine in my tray of small loaves as they bake through quickly and perfectly, and are just right to serve in small slices with a creamy, fruity dessert.

Delicious with chocolate ice-cream.

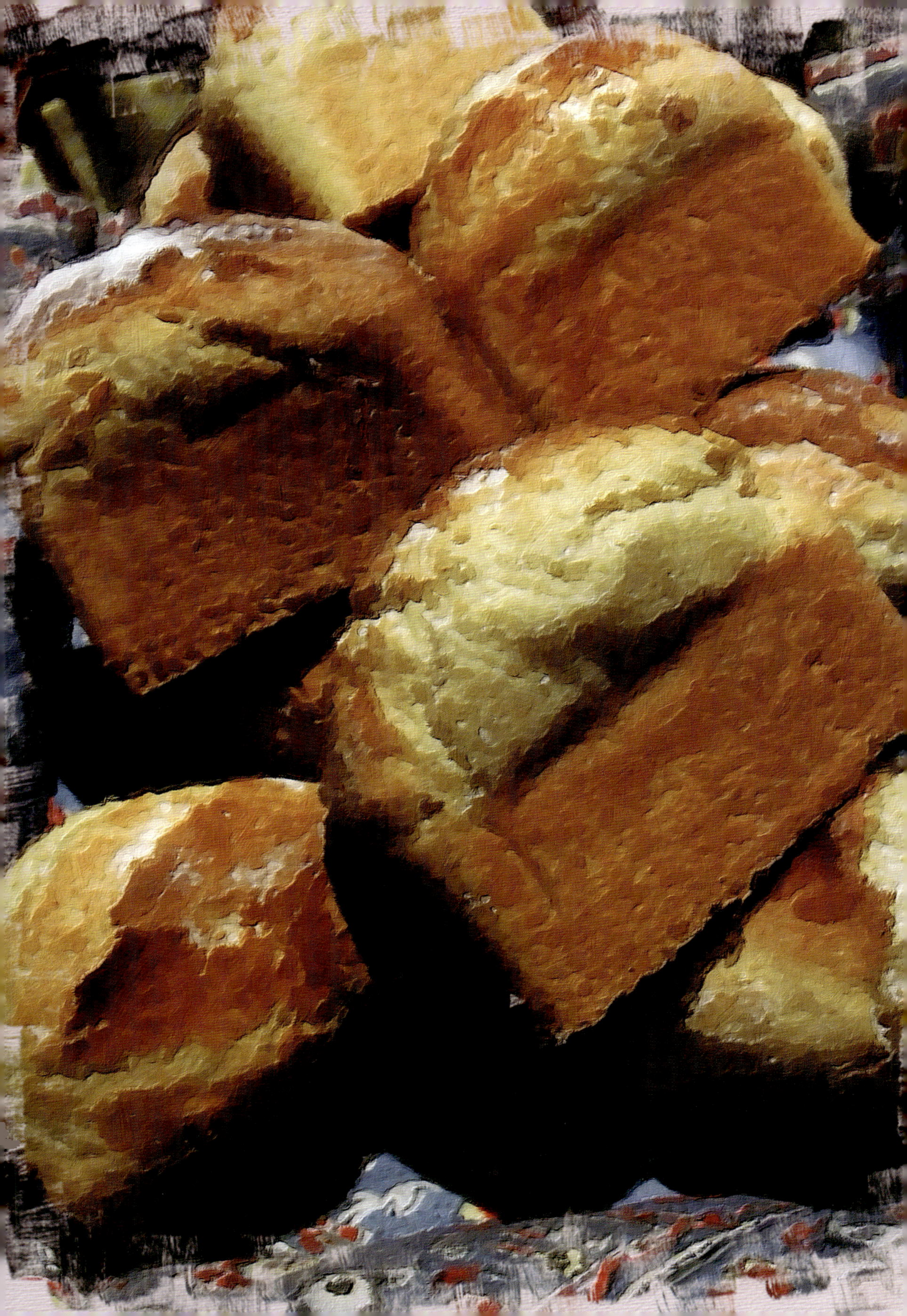

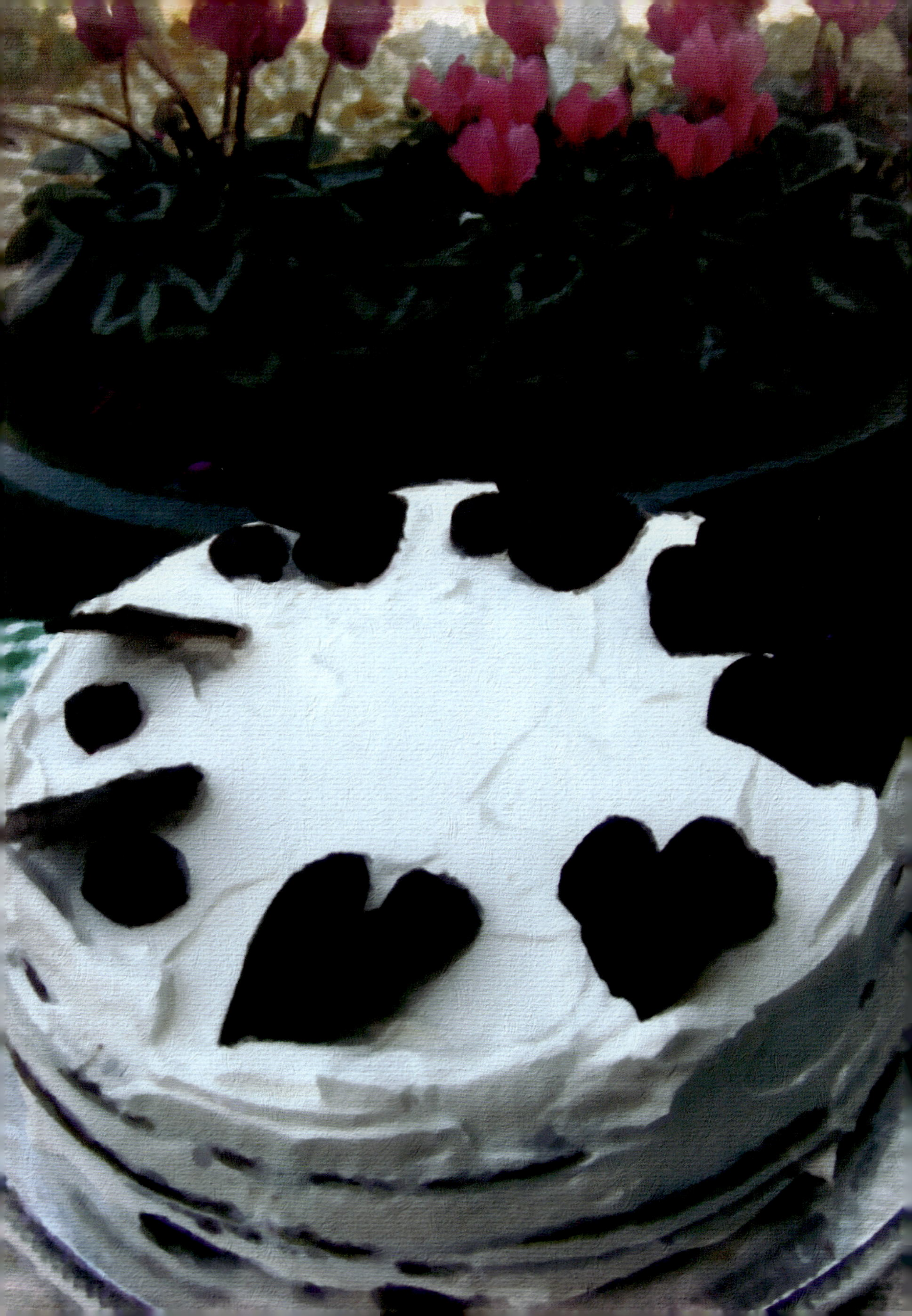

# Forêt Noire

*It is totally unreasonable that a very bad representation of this cake can be found in a supermarket deep freeze and even worse that it should be allowed to carry the name of this unique and very traditional of all French recipes.*

500g black cherries, the tins or jars are best (drained of the water)
100ml of kirsch
100g butter
6 eggs
100g caster sugar
75g ground almonds
60g cocoa powder
180g self-raising flour
1 tsp vanilla essence
20g dark chocolate
12 or so fresh cherries to decorate
   (or natural glacé cherries if fresh are not available)
300ml whipped cream with a little vanilla sugar added

Soak the cherries in the kirsch for 2 hours. Melt the butter without letting it take colour. Separate the eggs and to the lightly whisked yolks add the castor sugar, melted butter, ground almonds, cocoa powder, the flour and the vanilla. Mix until smooth. Whisk the egg whites until firm and fold carefully into the mixture with a spatula. Butter and line a 25cm cake tin and spread the mixture in, placing to bake in a moderately hot oven for 30minutes. Cool in the tin.

Cut the cake horizontally into 3 layers and drizzle with the liquid from the marinating cherries. Spread the cherries equally on two of the layers. Prepare the whipped cream and use ¾ of this to spread over the fruit. Assemble the cake and spread the whole with the rest of the whipped cream to make a thin covering. Melt the dark chocolate and spread onto baking parchment. When beginning to harden using a metal spatula dipped in hot water and dried, carefully make small sticks of chocolate to decorate the finished cake, adding the fresh cherries halved and stoned around the edge.

Chill for 2 hours before serving.

# Dacquoise aux Pistaches

*Dacquoise or meringue based cakes make the perfect dessert for long summer days in the garden. In fact as we have been treated to some real summer weather this June, I made 3 dacquiose for the shop this week, 1 peach and 2 raspberry and there is not a single piece left for me to eat whilst working on my cake book!*

*This recipe from the Landais is most definitely for a special occasion, the layers of delicate pistachio and almond meringue being assembled with a white chocolate mousse flavoured with Grand Marnier.*

**3 egg whites**
**20g caster sugar**
**40g ground almonds**
**40g ground pistachios**
**80g icing sugar**
**redcurrants and/or physalis for decoration**

**For the mousse:**
**180g white chocolate**
**2 egg yolks**
**2 leaves of gelatine**
**1 measure of Grand Marnier**
**300g whipped cream**

Whisk the egg whites and add the sugar as they begin to firm. When stiff add the ground nuts and icing sugar. Pipe 2 round layers of the meringue onto baking parchment and cook for 25 minutes in a moderately hot oven.

**To prepare the mousse:** Melt the chocolate in a bain-marie and spread about a tablespoonful on to baking parchment to make a decoration for the finished cake. Disolve the gelatine leaves in a bowl over hot water with a little water added to the Grand Marnier. Mix the egg yolks into the melted chocolate and add the dissolved gelatine. Fold in the whipped cream and chill until the mousse is set. Spread between the meringue layers keeping a little back to pipe a decoration on the top.

Decorate with the fruit and slivers of the white chocolate that was set aside.

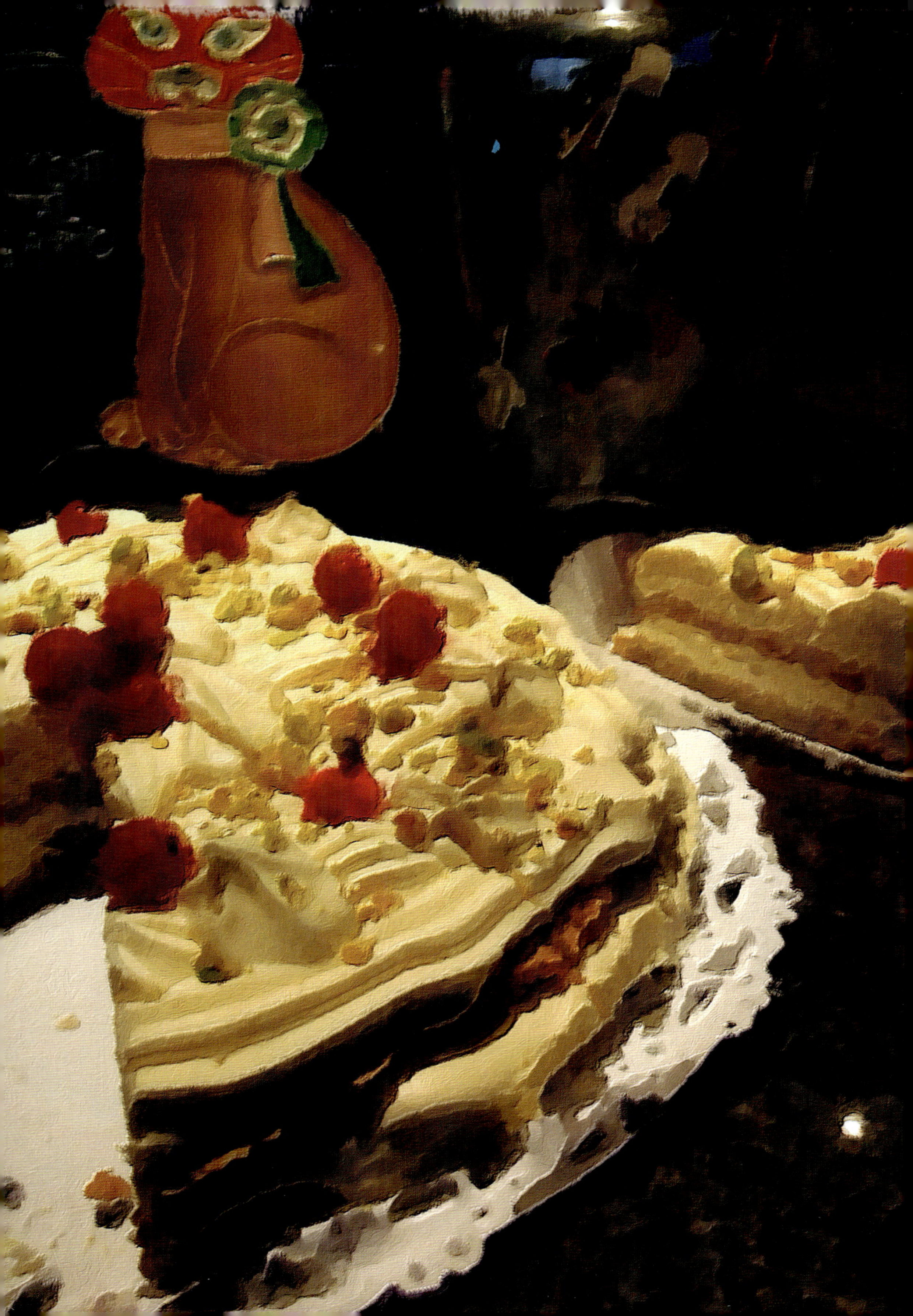

# CAKES WITH DRIED F

## TS, NUTS AND SEEDS

*Le Vieux Four's* **Lorimer Plum Cake with Guinness**

**Lemon Whiskey Cake**

**Kouglof**

**Seed cake**

**Hazelnut & Coffee Cake with Chocolate Sauce**

**Bara Brith**

**Nut Cake with Brandy**

**Earl Grey Tea Loaf**

# Le Vieux Four's Lorimer Plum Cake

My grandmother Jeanetta originally from New Zealand used to delight in recreating all sorts of different fruit cakes and we were invited subsequently for very a formal tea. I always went home with the most awful tummy ache and I put it down to the nervousness I felt on such occasions. It was some years later when I realised that all dried fruits have this effect on me, delicious although they are at the moment of consumption, and the pain I felt had nothing to do with the awe I felt in the presence of my rather stern paternal grandmother.

This cake definitely matures with keeping, in fact should be kept a week before cutting, and is wonderful with cheese on a picnic.

250g butter or marg
500g flour
300g dark brown sugar
250g currants
250g raisins
125g chopped candied peel
1 tsp mixed spice
250ml Guiness
grated rind ½ a lemon
4 eggs
1 tsp baking powder

**Topping:**
100g sugar
50g roughly chopped walnut pieces

Rub the fat into the flour, add the sugar, fruit, peel, spice and zest. Whisk the stout and add the beaten eggs and soda. Pour onto the other ingredients and mix well. Butter and line a 25cm deep cake tin or 2 loaf tins. and spread the mixture in. Bake in a moderate oven for 1½–2 hours.

**For the topping:** Melt the sugar in a heavy pan without stirring and allow to turn a golden brown. stir in the walnuts and quickly spread in the middle of your cake.

# Lemon Whiskey Cake

*A favourite cake years ago for shooting parties, the whiskey taking the flavour of lemon by the marination of the peel, is a unique touch for this mixture, guaranteed to warm up a simple picnic. As a child I used to holiday at my great-aunt and uncle's house, more of a castle really, called Dunderave. Situated near the village of Bushmills where they make what my mother assured me was 'the finest of all malt whiskey', I remember the Irish cook there making us the king of all picnics to eat on the sand dunes or on our wanderings to the Giants Causeway.*

3 eggs
200g caster sugar
200g self-raising flour
200g butter
1 large lemon
50ml whisky
200g sultanas

Peel the lemon thinly into strips and place these in a glass with the whisky on the preceding day. Cream the butter with the sugar and separate the eggs. Add the yolks one by one with a spoonful of flour in-between. Mix the sultanas into the mixture with the strained whisky and a little more of the flour. Whip the whites stiffly and fold in with the rest of the flour. Turn into a buttered and paper lined tin and bake in a moderate oven for 1–1½ hours. Cut the lemon strips finely and dry them tossed in caster sugar for decoration.

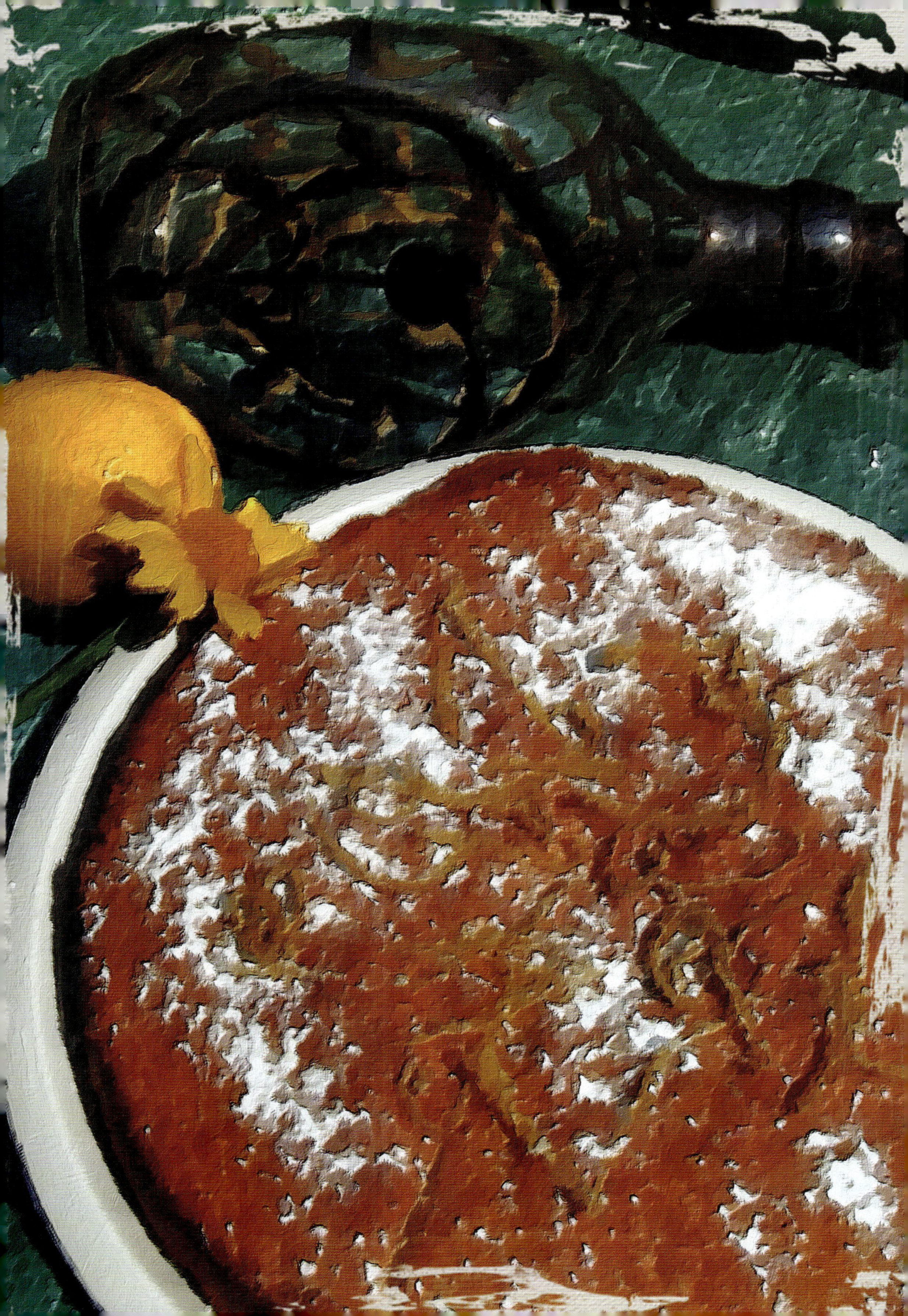

# Kouglof

*A recipe from Alsace, a little complicated but definitely a triumph when brought to the table for a festive occasion.*

100g raisins
500g flour
1 sachet of easy bake yeast
50g flaked almonds
40g butter
20g icing sugar
2 eggs
150ml warm milk
½ tsp salt
100g caster sugar
150g butter

Soak the raisins in water for a few hours until they are swollen, and then strain. Place the flour, yeast, salt and sugar in the bowl of your mixer and making a well in the centre, add the eggs, and milk and mix all together until the dough pulls away from the sides of the bowl. Gradually incorporate the butter and the raisins. Cover and leave to prove in a warm place for an hour or until doubled in size. Butter a fluted mould, flour lightly and scatter with flaked almonds. Knock the dough down and place in the mould, leaving to prove again for another hour and a half. Cook in a moderately hot oven for 45minutes.

Turn out the Kouglof and brush with cooled melted butter and sprinkle with icing sugar.

# Seed Cake

*French patisserie can be so grand and fancy but it takes a lot to beat the old fashioned British cakes that our ancestors have baked for centuries, being not glamorous at all but full of sustenance and goodness.*

250g flour
250g butter
250g caster sugar
5 eggs
50g candied peel

pinch nutmeg
1 tsp caraway seeds
2 tbsp brandy
crushed brown crystal coffee sugar

Beat the butter with the sugar until creamy. Separate the eggs and beat in the yolks one by one alternately with a teaspoon of flour between each addition. Add the peel, the nutmeg, the caraway seeds and fold in the stiffly beaten egg whites and the remaining flour. Lastly stir in the brandy and place in a buttered and lined 25cm tin. Bake in the centre of a moderate oven for 1 hour.

Decorate with the crushed sugar, brushing the cake with a little hot jam to make it stick.

# Hazelnut & Coffee Cake with Chocolate Sauce

*Often we mix coffee with walnuts, but try this idea with a chocolate sauce, or replace the cream in the middle with apples softly poached with lemon and some apricot jam to produce an extraordinarily good cake.*

200g butter
200g soft light brown sugar
2 eggs plus 2 whites
100g ground hazelnuts
200g self-raising flour
lightly whipped double cream for the filling
1 tbsp good strong espresso
2 tbsp milk

For the chocolate sauce:
200g best dark chocolate
2 tbsp coffee
1 tbsp rum
40g butter

For the alternative apple filling:
500g bramleys
1 lemon
2 tbsp apricot jam

Bake the hazelnuts until they brown, and by rubbing them in a clean tea towel remove the skins, as they would impart a bitter flavour to the cake. In a food processor grind them to breadcrumb size. Cream the butter with the sugar, and beat in the eggs, nuts, flour and coffee, stir in the milk. Whisk the egg whites until stiff and fold them in to the mixture carefully.

Bake in 2 greased sandwich tins, or one large cake tin with the intention of halving the cake to fill, in a moderate oven until firm to the touch.

Fill when cold with softly whipped cream, or apple.

**For the sauce:** Melt the chocolate over hot water and add the butter followed by the flavourings.

**For the apple filling:** Peel, core and thickly slice the apples and place in a pan with the grated rind and juice of the lemon and the jam. Cook fairly quickly until just soft, shaking the pan to prevent the apples from disintegrating, and cool before filling the cake.

# Bara Brith

*Strictly speaking this is a fruit bread, but where one draws the line between cake and bread is hard to tell, except maybe the use of yeast instead of baking powder as the raising agent in the recipe makes it come under the heading of bread. Bara Brith can be bought in shops in Wales where the recipe was born but the commercially produced version leaves plenty to be desired. The following rich version is delicious sliced and spread with creamy, unsalted butter and definitely brings something special to any tea table.*

*Elizabeth David tells us that many of these English yeast dough specialities were simply a spin off from the weekly bread baking, a portion of the dough being kept aside to create something sweet in time for tea, which seems a very logical reason for their evolution.*

*If you feel like adding a very specialist touch, you can mix your own mixed spice and I have added an old French formula for 'epices douces' at the foot of this recipe, which if stored in a jar can be used in other recipes that call for a mixed spice blend.*

'Epices Douces' from La Varenne's 'Patissier François' first published in 1655:
2 parts ground ginger to one each of pepper, cloves, nutmeg and cinnamon.

450g flour
1 sachet easy bake yeast
85g butter
150ml milk
80g soft brown sugar
100g currants
100g raisins
30g chopped soft dried apricots
1 tsp mixed sweet spice
1 egg
½ tsp salt

Soak the raisins and currants in cold tea to plump them, and strain away the surplus liquid.

Place yeast, flour and salt in a warm bowl. Warm the milk with the butter and beat in the egg. Mix into the flour to form a light dough. Cover and leave to rise for 1 hour at room temperature. Warm the fruits, sugar and spice and work into the dough, if it seems too stiff add a little more milk.

Pat into shape and place in a warm buttered loaf tin and prove again until risen to the top of the tin.

Bake in the centre of a moderately hot oven for 20–30 minutes covering with foil for the last 10, to protect the crust. Leave to cool before turning out.

*Fruits, Nuts & Seeds*

# Nut Cake with Brandy

*Deliciously nutty, a cake to be made in the autumn and decorated with hazelnuts picked freshly and still in their greenish, brown husks.*

120g ground roast nuts
   (an almond and hazelnut mix)
4 eggs
200g soft brown sugar
200g butter
100g self-raising flour

For the drizzle:
50g sugar
4 tbsp water
2 tbsp brandy

Beat butter and sugar together until creamy, add the eggs alternately with the dry ingredients until well mixed.

Butter and line a 25cm mould and bake in a moderately hot oven for 40 minutes.

Dissolve the sugar in water for the drizzle, boiling until syrupy. Add the brandy and pour over the warm cake.

*Fruits, Nuts & Seeds* 93

# Earl Grey Tea Loaf with Caramelised Almonds & Lemon Cream

*Perfect to accompany and compliment all those scented, gentle teas: Lapsang, Chai or Darjeeling and of course Earl Grey that I have used to flavour the loaf itself. Bake the cake as a loaf or in small muffins, equally as good and enchanting piped with the lemon cream.*

250g sugar
100g of blanched flaked almonds
70ml of Earl Grey tea
230g butter
4 eggs
230g self-raising flour

For the lemon cream:
1 egg plus 4 yolks
75g sugar
100ml freshly squeezed lemon juice
60g butter
150ml double cream

To caramelise the almonds, heat 50g of the sugar with 1½ tbsp water until reaching a light caramel colour. Stir in the almonds and tip onto a baking sheet, setting aside until completely cold.

Infuse the tea and leave to cool.

Mix together butter, flour and eggs and add the cold tea. Stir in the broken pieces of almond caramel, reserving some to decorate the finished loaf. Place in two small lined loaf tins and bake in a moderate oven until risen and firm.

**For the lemon cream:** Whisk the egg yolks and whole egg with the sugar. Heat the lemon juice in a saucepan and pour onto the egg and sugar mixture, stirring well. Heat in the saucepan until it almost boils stirring all the time and then add the butter in dice off the heat, mixing thoroughly. Allow to cool before adding the whipped cream and pipe the icing carefully onto the loaves, decorating finally with the remaining almonds either whole or processed to a chunky praline.

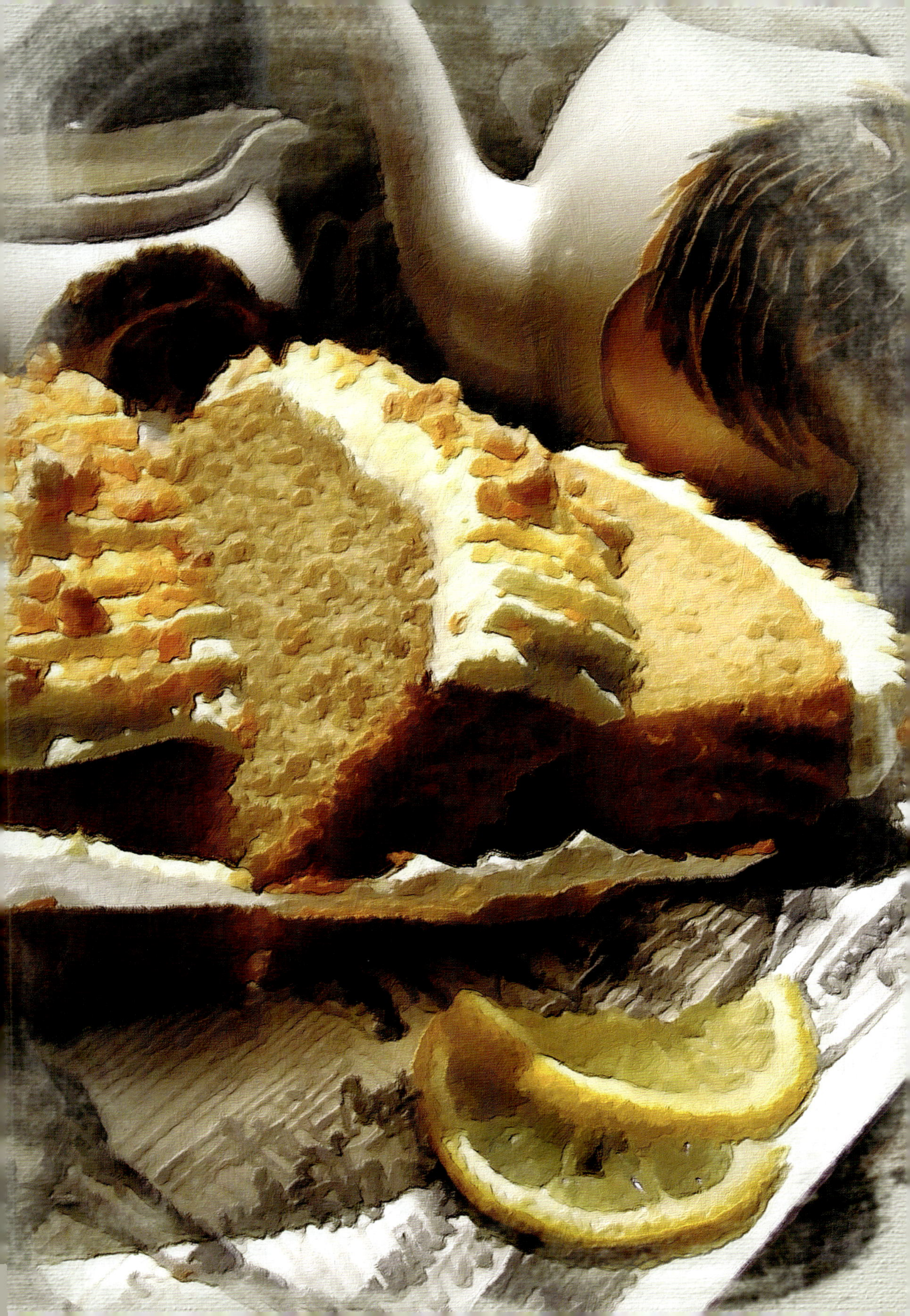

# LE VIEUX FOUR SIMPLE

*In these recipes I have tried to include a variation of that you will experiment to adding flavours to the ch pepper or a favo*

ered him wholesale and on-trade, reflecting the rise of whisky's popularity in the mid-1800s.

# ...CH CHOCOLATE CAKES

...niques involved in successful cake baking and hope
...ate that suit your personal taste, for example chilli,
...liquor or spice

**Chocolate, Cocoa & Almond Cake**

**Very Chocolatey Dark Chocolate Cake**

**Chocolate Cake with Rum**

**Chocolate Cake with Espresso & Ground Almonds**

**Chocolate Crown**

**Brownies with Pistachio & Pepper Cream Sauce**

# Chocolate, Cocoa & Almond Cake

*This cake is based more on the method of a traditional genoise, but baked in a bain-marie to slow down the baking process and produce a wonderful texture to the finished cake. If the cake sinks in the middle do not worry, it is perfect.*

125g dark chocolate
4 eggs
1 tbsp cornflour
100g sugar
2 tbsp cocoa powder
80g soft butter
pinch of salt
1 tbsp flour
50g flaked almonds

Melt the chocolate in a double boiler.

Separate the yolks and the whites of the eggs, and work the former with the sugar until creamy and white. Add the cornflour, cocoa, melted chocolate and butter.

Whip the egg whites until firm peaks, and fold carefully into the mixture. Butter and line a cake mould, a square one works well for this, and spreading the mixture in and bake in a moderate oven in a bain-marie for 50 minutes.

Take the cake from the tin to cool and sprinkle with toasted flaked almonds and cocoa powder.

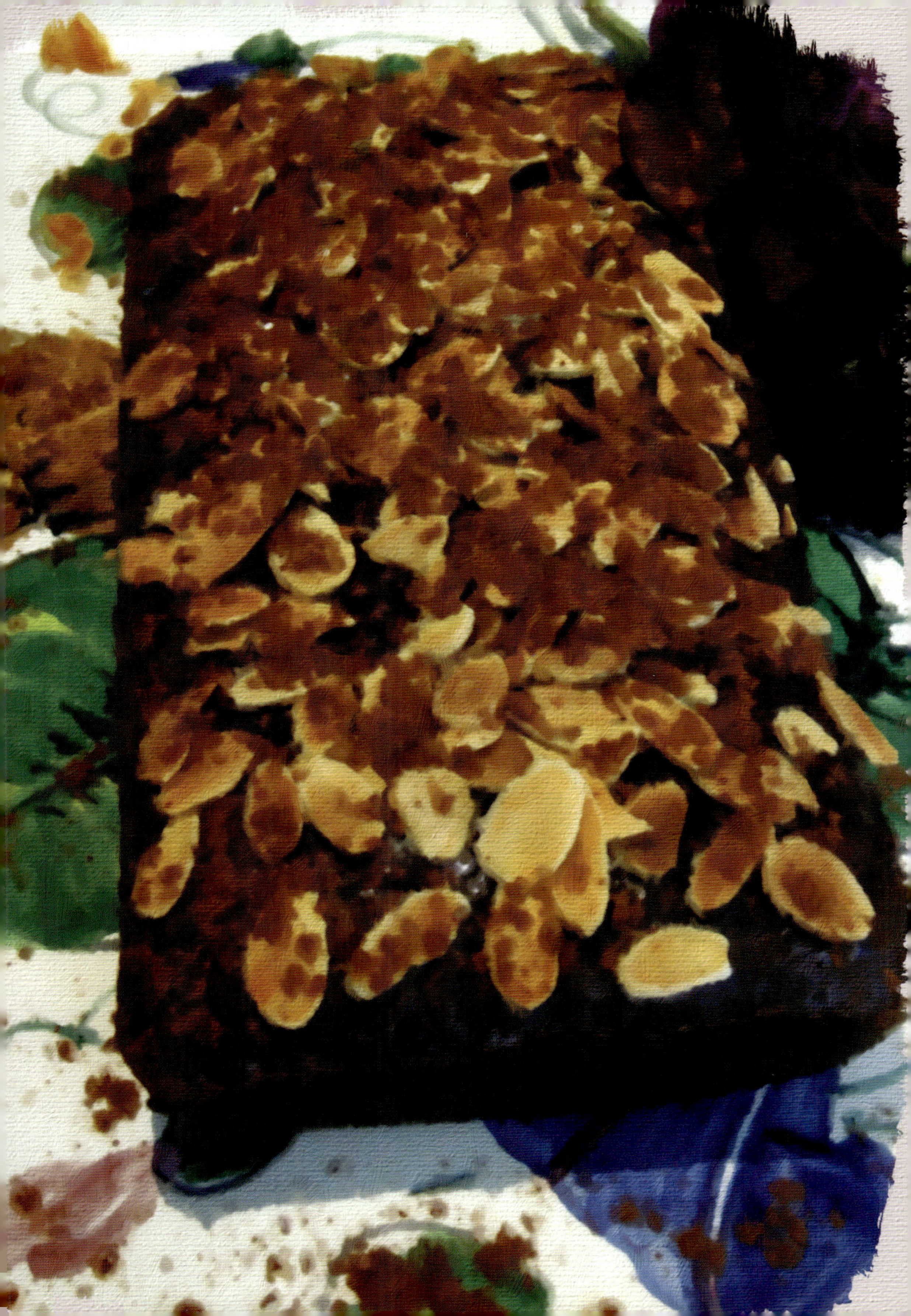

# Very Chocolatey Dark Chocolate Cake

*This recipe is very similar to my chocolate brownie recipe that is, of course, included in my first book. Baked in a pretty mould, with again a slightly gooey middle, this makes a wonderful centrepiece to teatime.*

200g finest dark chocolate
200g butter
160g sugar
4 eggs

150g self-raising flour
20g cocoa
icing sugar to sprinkle

Melt the chocolate with the butter until smooth over a gentle heat. Remove the pan from the flame and add the sugar and eggs. Mix in the sieved flour and cocoa until smooth. Butter and flour lightly a cake mould such as you would use for a brioche or similar, and bake the mixture for 15 or 20 minutes in a moderate oven. Un-mould the cake and serve warm sprinkled with icing sugar.

Delicious as a pudding with crème patissière.

*Simple Rich Chocolate Cakes* **101**

# Chocolate Cake with Rum

*Of course I would try a chocolate cake with Mount Gay rum, just my favourite tipple ever! A butter-free cake.*

4 eggs
200g sugar
200g grated dark chocolate
20cl crème fraîche
200g sieved self-raising flour

2 tbsp Mount Gay rum
a pinch of grated nutmeg
1 tsp freshly grated orange zest
icing sugar to sprinkle

Beat the eggs and adding the sugar, continue to beat over hot water in a double boiler until the mixture becomes thick. Take from the heat, place the mix in a bowl and add the chocolate, followed by the crème fraîche and the flour, stirring carefully with a wooden spoon. Finally stir in the rum. Butter and line a 25cm tin and bake in a moderately hot oven for 30 mins. A blade inserted in this cake should come out clean when it is done.

Serve when completely cooled.

This cake is delicious sliced in two horizontally and filled with chocolate crème patisserie.

*Simple Rich Chocolate Cakes* 103

# Chocolate Cake with Espresso & Ground Almonds

The final one in this little collection of variations, again based on the theme of chocolate flavoured whisked cake. Dressed up or dressed down this is a truly delicious standby for a special tea of after dinner treat and despite its upside down method, it works beautifully every time.

4 eggs
150g sugar
200g dark chocolate
1 tbsp strong espresso coffee
2 tbsp self-raising flour
100g ground almonds
150g soft butter
pinch of salt

Separate the eggs, and mix the yolks with the sugar until white and creamy. Melt the chocolate in a double boiler and add the coffee. Mix into the yolks and sugar, and add the flour, almonds and the butter cut into dice, stirring constantly until smooth. Whisk the whites to firm peaks with the salt and fold into the cake mix carefully.

Turn into a buttered and lined 24cm mould and bake in a hot oven for 20 minutes, leaving to cool completely before turning out and serving.

# Chocolate Crown

*Once mastered a chocolate genoise bakes beautifully in a crown shape if you can find a fluted crown tin such as one might use for a baba. With a rich chocolate ganache icing and decorated with exotic fruits, this makes a wonderful centrepiece for an occasion or festive table.*

4 eggs
150g sugar
150g butter
150g dark chocolate
80g self-raising flour
2 tbsp brandy
fruits to decorate

Ganache icing:
130cl double cream
200g dark chocolate

Separate the eggs and whites and work with the sugar until white and creamy. Melt the butter with the chocolate over a gentle heat or in a double boiler. Mix this in with the yolk–sugar combination and fold in the flour and cognac. Whisk the egg whites to firm peaks and stir carefully into the mixture. Butter and flour lightly a 22cm crown mould and bake for 25 minutes in a moderately hot oven, until risen and firm to the touch.

**For the ganache:** Heat the cream until almost boiling and add the chocolate in small pieces. Mix over the heat for a minute or so and continue to stir until smooth. Leave to thicken and cool a little before icing your crown.

Physalis make the perfect decoration for this cake.

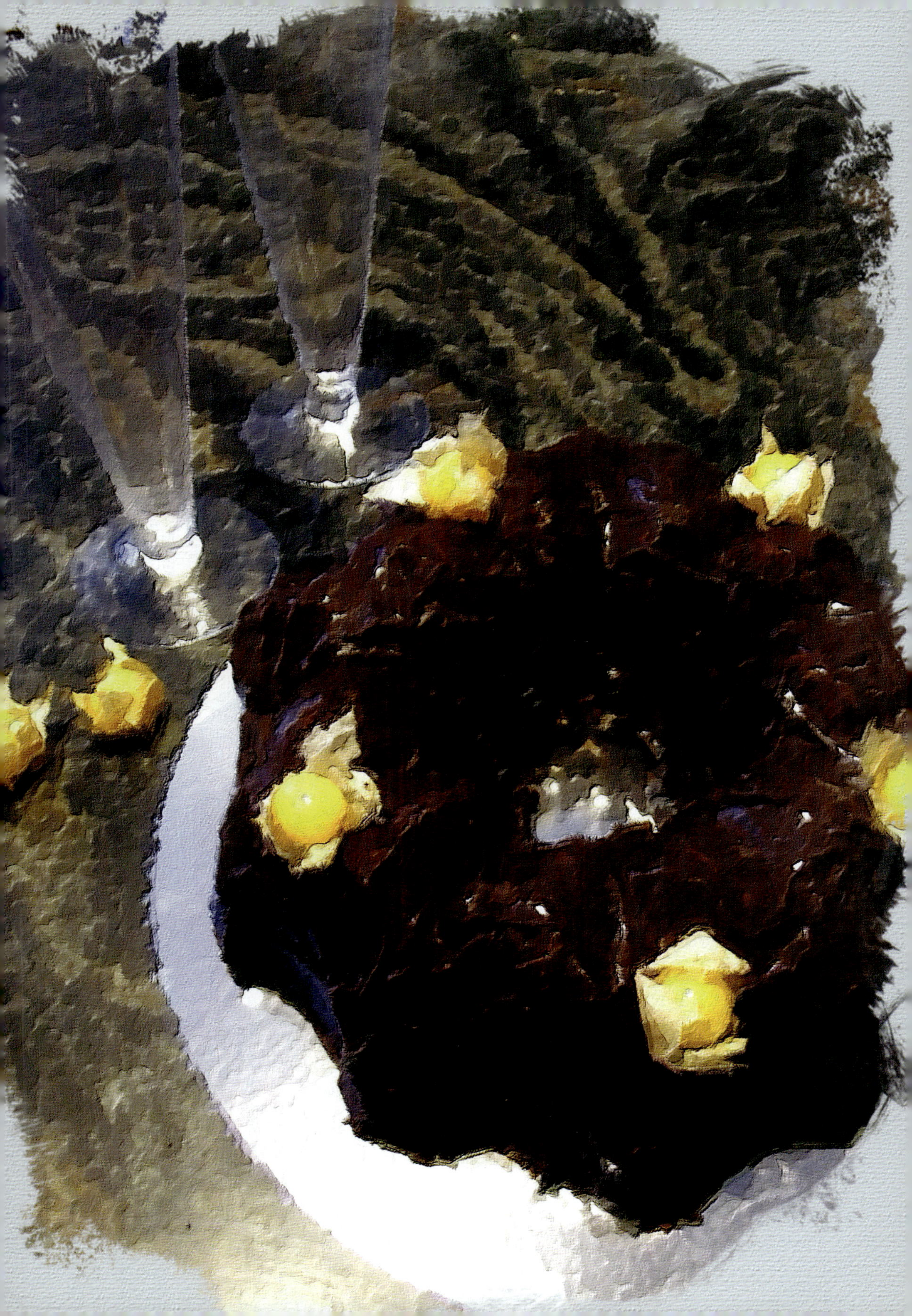

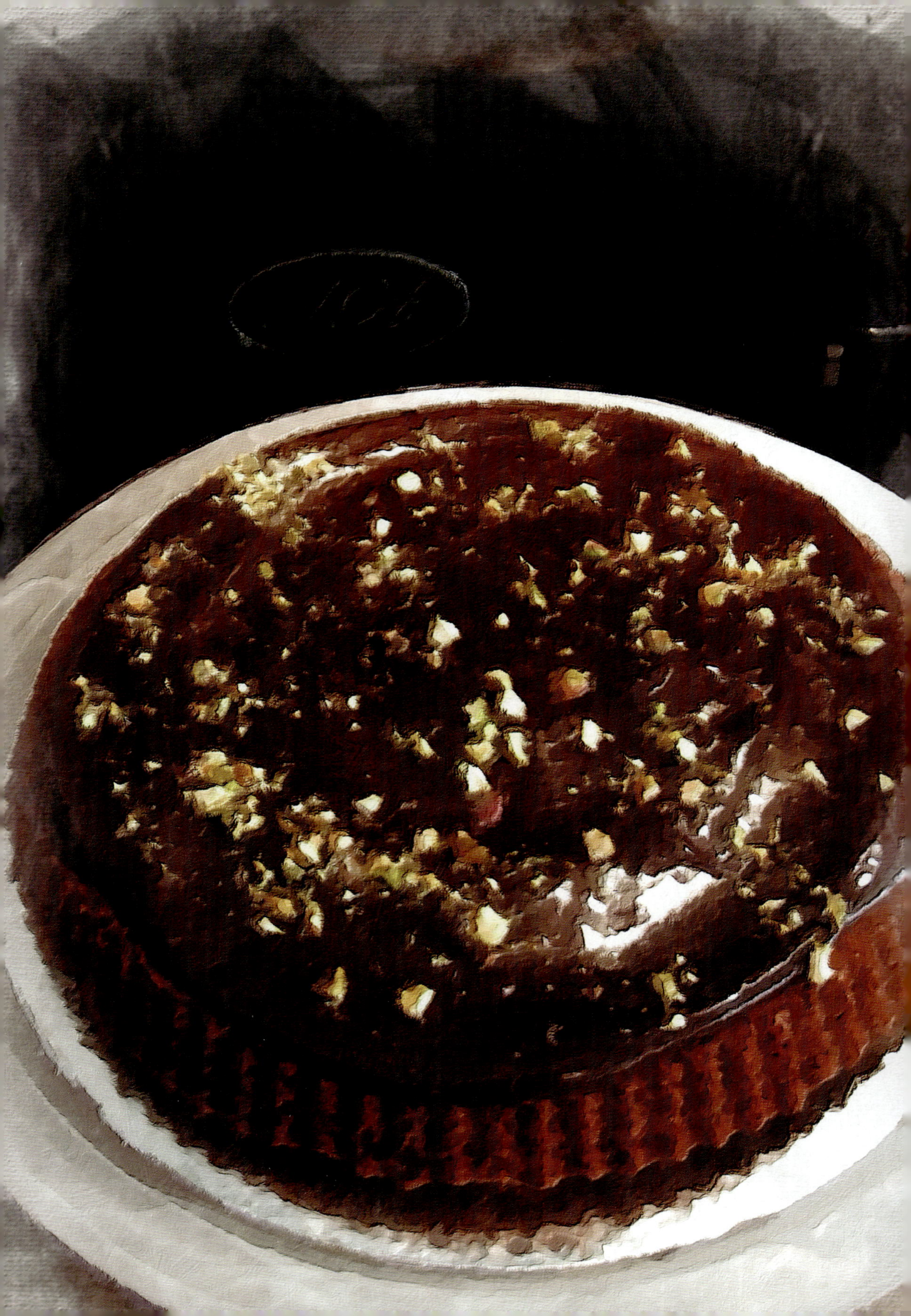

# Brownies with Pistachio & Pepper Cream Sauce

*The ultimate twist on my brownie recipe to please those who like to ring the changes, but I think there would be disapproval if I tried to substitute these for my 'everyday brownies' at Le Vieux Four, perhaps once in a while…*

60g dark chocolate
120g butter
180g sugar
2 eggs
4 tbsp self-raising flour
100g chopped pistachios

For the pepper cream:
30g sugar
2 egg yolks
3 tbsp double cream
3 peppercorns
50g melted dark or white chocolate

Melt the chocolate in a double boiler and mix in the butter, sugar and eggs. Stir in the flour and pistachios. Spread into a lined baking tray, the mix should be about 5cm in depth.

Bake in a moderately hot oven for about 30 minutes, the centre should stay a bit soft and moist as for traditional brownies.

**To make the pepper cream icing:** Whisk the sugar with the egg yolks until white and creamy. In a saucepan bring the milk to the boil with the cream and the crushed peppercorns, and pour this over the egg yolk and sugar mix, whisking as you pour. Bring this mixture back to the heat and cook until coating the back of the wooden spoon. Sieve and stir in the melted chocolate. When the icing thickens spread carefully on the cake.

# Bibliography

*Larousse Gastrominique*, Prosper Montagne; Hamlyn 1961

*Les Desserts*; Solar 2001

*The Constance Spry Cookery Book*, Constance Spry and Rosemary Hume; J. M. Dent and Sons 1957

*English Bread and Yeast Cookery*, Elizabeth David; Penguin Books 1986

PhotoArtista oil v2.09 used to develop photos to resemble oil paintings.

# Index of Distinctive Ingredients

almond  6, 10, 16, 24, 37, 38, 42, 44, 64, 68, 75, 76, 84, 92, 94, 98, 104
anis  10
apple  4, 34, 44, 88
apricot  6, 38, 58, 91
    jam  14, 38, 88

banana  18
blackberry  44
Black Cow vodka  2
blueberry  28, 55
brandy  86, 92, 106

caraway  86
cherry  xii, 14, 42, 64, 75
chocolate, dark  12, 31, 75, 88, 98, 100, 102, 104, 106, 109
chocolate, white  2, 31, 76, 109
cinnamon  8, 10, 14, 18, 34, 50, 52, 56, 90
cloves  10, 90
coffee  12, 88, 104
coriander  10
cornflour  48, 62, 98
cranberries  4

fennel  58
fig  22

gelatine  10, 76
ginger  10, 48, 50, 56, 90
golden syrup  50
grape  41
guiness  xiii, 80

hazelnut  8, 37, 54, 88, 92

kirsch  24, 41, 75

lavender  16
lemon  14, 16, 28, 32, 63, 70, 80, 82, 88, 94

marzipan  4, 37
mascarpone  50
Mount Gay rum  4, 18, 42, 52, 102

nutmeg  4, 14, 18, 50, 52, 56, 86, 90, 102

orange flower water  56, 72

papaya  18
pear  8
pineapple  31
plum  24, 48, 80
praline  6, 68, 94
prune  2, 48
pumpkin seeds  56

raspberries  28, 32, 37, 50
rhubarb  26, 32
rice  38

sunflower seeds  56

yeast  41, 66, 70, 72, 84, 90

*Index*  **111**

# Recipe Notes